Powdermills

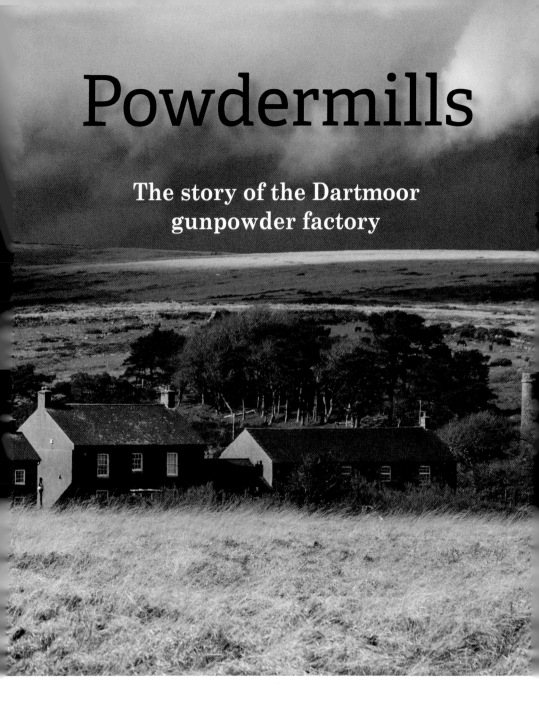

Powdermills

The story of the Dartmoor gunpowder factory

Drew Campbell

Foreword by Tom Greeves

BLACKINGSTONE
PUBLISHING

Dedication
For Amelie and Jude

First published 2019
Published for Drew Campbell by Blackingstone Publishing
2 Steward Cottages Moretonhampstead Devon TQ13 8SD

Contemporary photographs by Dianne Jayne Giles

Edited by Sue Viccars www.dartmoormagazine.co.uk
Designed by Emily Kingston

ISBN 978-0-9954986-1-7

Typesetting and origination by Blackingstone Publishing
Printed in Great Britain by Short Run Press, Exeter, Devon

Acknowledgements
Many thanks are due to the following: Professor Keith Snell for providing me with
the analytical tools needed to carry out this kind of research; Dr Richard Jones for
his inspiring lectures and fun chats on all subjects including water history; Professor
Harold Fox (sadly no longer with us) for introducing me to Dartmoor; Joss Hibbs for
her enthusiasm for the project and great anecdotes; Dianne Giles for her amazing
photography; Bob Ashford for sharing his research and taking me on numerous tours
of the site where he had to explain the science of gunpowder production to the most
unscientific of students; Tom Stratton at the Duchy of Cornwall Office, Princetown;
Christy Rice for reading through my manuscript and finding numerous errors; Dr Katy
Layton Jones for reading through my many drafts and fixing my clunky writing style;
Helen Harris for her correspondence on the subject; Dr Tom Greeves who allowed
me to publish photos from his collection and kindly read and corrected my chapters
and provided much needed encouragement; Rita of Clipartqueen for her silhouettes;
Roderick Martin, Dr Steve Childs, Neil Mattingly, Keith Ryan, Adrian Taylor, Richard Paul
Wilson, David Grange and Richard Sambrook for access to their research and photos;
Terry Rounsefell for his analysis of the company partnerships; Netty for her artwork;
Sue Viccars and Emily Kingston from Blackingstone Publishing for their patience and
professionalism and finally Penny Campbell for her illustrations and for understanding
my need to engage in this sort of distraction.

Front cover PHOTOGRAPH DIANNE JAYNE GILES
Back cover Extract from a map of the site THE DUCHY ARCHIVES, PRINCETOWN

CONTENTS

FOREWORD

Travelling between Two Bridges and Postbridge it is impossible not to be seduced by one of the most enticing views on central Dartmoor – a row of sturdy granite cottages with coniferous and other trees masking a tall granite chimney stack and other buildings, framed against the dramatic backdrop of Longaford and other tors. This was the site of an enterprise by the Plymouth and Dartmoor Gunpowder Company for some fifty years from 1844, employing scores of workers, many of whom lived on site with their families.

Within the 33ha complex, the clean lines and massive construction of three wheelhouses on the east bank of the Cherrybrook, and a second well-preserved circular stack plus various ruins, are intriguing. The site is now nationally recognised as one of the finest in the country to have survived from the nineteenth century, producing gunpowder for mines and quarries on Dartmoor and beyond.

For the first time, the human story of Powdermills is presented in some detail in this book by Drew Campbell, drawing particularly on newly researched material in newspapers and archives. Not only are the employees revealed, but also their experiences of working and living in such a place in the mid-nineteenth century, with the constant risk of fatal explosions (several of which took place). The various roles and characters of owners, partners in the business, shareholders and agents are told within the context of the Victorian world and its ethos.

The author became 'captivated' by Powdermills, which he has now brought to life with much new data. Richly illustrated, fully sourced, and including a guide to the site itself, this book is a fine addition to our understanding of such a remarkable place of industry on Victorian Dartmoor.

Tom Greeves
Tavistock, March 2019

About the author

In the late nineties the record company IRS – owned by Miles Copeland, Sting's manager – went bust, and its artists found themselves unemployed. One of these musicians was Drew Campbell, who discovered that even though he no longer had a record deal he still had some of his advance. Rather than give the money to his local pub landlord he bought a narrowboat and took up 'duck watching'.

Sue Viccars and Drew Campbell at Powdermills, May 2019 PHOTOGRAPH DIANNE JAYNE GILES

After a year of observing the canal's waterfowl he got bored and decided to get an education. He enrolled part-time with the Open University and six years later was awarded a BA (Hons) in Humanities with Ancient History. He began studying part-time for his masters at Leicester University and after three years was awarded an MA in English Local History, with his dissertation wining the Richard McKinley and the John Nichols prizes.

Following a brief period of further duck observation Drew began studying for his PhD under the supervision of Professor Keith Snell. In 2012 he was awarded a doctorate for his research on the very canal on which his boat was floating.

Drew is now on dry land but still actively engaged in historical research. He lives in Hatherleigh in Devon with his wife Penny, their two children Amelie and Jude, and his cat Mr Boosh.

A note from the author

In 2012 I said goodbye to fifteen years of living on a narrowboat on the Ashby Canal, and with my pregnant wife Penny and our five-year-old daughter Amelie we left the Midlands for new adventures in Devon. In need of another research project to keep me out of trouble I turned my attention to Dartmoor, but what to study?[1] As most of my post-graduate research had focused on the history of water management (canals mostly), I began investigating how the harnessing of water not only affected the people of Dartmoor, but also the landscape.[2]

A few years into the project I visited a site known as Powdermills – mainly because someone (I cannot remember who) told me that the derelict gunpowder factory near Postbridge provided an excellent example of water management on Dartmoor. So in 2015 I found myself entering a large area of abandoned buildings, trackways, wheelpits and chimneys, and I was completely captivated. Clearly this was once a busy place, where many people had invested time and effort in these structures, but then for some reason they were left to fall into disrepair. I wandered from building to building trying to make sense of how the site worked, but it was beyond me. However, I could see evidence of water power being used, as many of the buildings had large pits for waterwheels.

Rain stopped play that day – as it often does on Dartmoor – and I retreated to the nearby Powdermills Pottery. Over coffee in the gallery, I quizzed the resident potter and proprietor Joss Hibbs about the factory. She informed me that 'gunpowder was produced here for about fifty years, and there has been some research carried out on the place, but we know very little about the people who worked and lived here'. Joss further explained how the nearby row of cottages (still in use today) were originally built for the company employees, and that the building we sat in was believed to be either a chapel or a school for the workers' children.

Enthused by my visit I began some preliminary investigations just to see if anything else could be discovered. It didn't take long for the stories to begin leaping out of the torn and worn pages of various documents (mostly old newspapers and census reports): tales of workers running off with the managers' daughters, explosions causing death and injury, assaults, court cases, damning factory inspections, poetry-writing workers and even a connection to 'Jack the Ripper'. I also learned that a large number of children lived on the site and that, as Joss had mentioned, a school was built especially for them. I was completely captivated and decided that the story of the people of Powdermills had to be told.

It has taken a number of years to research and write this book. To those who find it hard to understand why we should put so much effort into learning about 'a load of dead people' I offer the following statement by the historian Arthur Marwick:

> The simplest answer to the questions 'Why do history?' or 'What is the use of history?' is: 'Try to imagine what it would be like living in a society in which there was absolutely no knowledge of the past.' The mind boggles. It is only through a sense of history that communities establish their identities, orientate themselves, understand their relationship to the past and to other communities and societies. Without history (knowledge of the past), we, and our communities, would be utterly adrift on an endless and featureless sea of time.[3]

Obviously I agree with the above sentiments (who wouldn't), but for me there were additional motives for carrying out this research. Truth is, I love the escapism that historical research provides and more than anything I find spending time focusing on other people (even though they are dead) gives me a well-earned break from myself.

INTRODUCTION

I believe that a balanced and rounded appreciation of the past enhances our respect for humanity, both dead and alive.

Francis Pryor, archaeologist[4]

In the middle of Dartmoor, between Two Bridges and Postbridge, lie the extensive ruins of a gunpowder-making factory known as Powdermills. Having operated between 1845 and 1897, it has lain abandoned for well over a hundred years, and the buildings and chimneys of this once profitable human endeavour are now putting up a good fight against the forces of nature. Nevertheless, with each passing year these structures lose a little to the weathering of wind, water and sun and the smothering impact of vegetation, in particular gorse.[5] It is difficult not to be caught up in the atmosphere of this special place, and before long nagging questions begin to gnaw at an inquiring mind:

- In whose footsteps am I following?
- Who owned this factory?
- What sort of people worked here?
- Where did the people who were employed here live?
- What was the experience of working here?
- Was it a profitable venture – and if so, why did it stop?
- How did they make such a volatile product, and what were the risks?

Our knowledge of Powdermills has been greatly advanced by numerous studies, including those by Helen Harris, Andrew Pye, Rosemary Robinson, Frank Booker, Phil Newman, Alan Brunton, Eric Hemery and more recently Bob Ashford.[6] The science behind the process of gunpowder production and recent archaeological evidence has been dealt with by previous publications, and so this book will focus on the people connected to the gunpowder-making company and try to establish what it was like to work at the factory. It will also consider the politics involved in promoting, constructing and operating the works. Adrian Leftwich wrote that 'politics is at the heart of all collective social activity, formal and informal, public and private, in all human groups, institutions and societies',[7] and with this in mind this book traces and reconstructs the production of gunpowder on Dartmoor through the buildings, census returns, chancery court records, correspondence with

The earliest known photograph of the site c.1900, showing the buildings still roofed
TOM GREEVES COLLECTION

the Duchy Office and newspaper reports. The results of these enquiries will hopefully provide us with a greater understanding of the human story behind the Powdermills' structures – the challenges, the disputes, the successes, the failures, the factions and the finances.

CHAPTER 1
A worker's day

We should never advise anyone, who is not called by duty, to visit a Powder Factory, for firstly you run the risk of being blown to nothing, and, secondly you increase the danger in which the workmen are placed.

Godey's Lady's Book 1861[8]

So what was it like, living and working at Powdermills? Unfortunately no personal accounts – letters, diaries and so on – belonging to the company's employees have survived. Nevertheless, by piecing together what little we know (from official records, folklore and newspaper accounts) with research carried out on nineteenth-century families, work practices and other gunpowder mills, it's possible to get some idea of what the average worker experienced.

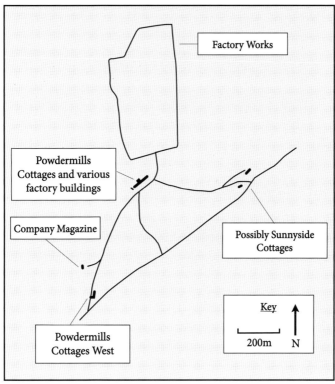

Plan of the factory site and accommodation

At work

For a Dartmoor powder worker the answer to the question 'How was your day?' was dependent on many different factors including the nature of his work, his shift, whether he lived on- or off-site, the current structure of ownership (see Chapter 2), the safety practices carried out by himself and his colleagues, the weather and the inevitable politics that occur in every workplace.[9] Breakfast for most employees was bread and tea.[10] One humorous exception was the Cornish-born Silas Sleep, a powder labourer who lived in Postbridge. Silas is documented as having claimed that he ate his breakfast and dinner together in the morning just in case he got blown up in the course of the working day and missed a meal.[11]

Silas Sleep (left), a factory worker, with his father James c.1890s TOM GREEVES COLLECTION

Having eaten breakfast, the factory employees left their homes to go to work. A large proportion of the workforce lived on-site at Powdermills Cottages, Powdermills Cottages West or Sunnyside Cottages.[12] However, many people lived off-site and had to walk to work, as revealed by the first census to record the factory's workforce in 1851 (Table 1). For the inhabitants of Cherrybrook and Cherrybrook Bridge the distance was less than a mile, but for the workers from Postbridge a walk of 2½ miles taking on average fifty minutes was required. No wonder Silas Sleep chose to eat two meals before setting off! Having made similar journeys in the rain that so frequently falls upon the moor, locals can well appreciate how difficult it must have been to then do a day's work when soaked through.

Eric Hemery explains how when George Stephens' grandfather worked at the Powdermills:

> George's grandmother often walked from Postbridge to the mills especially to take
> her husband a hot, newly-baked pasty for his dinner, they meeting by arrangement
> at the entrance-gate, for admittance to all but the workers was strictly forbidden.[13]

Remarkably the 1861 census records three 'powdermill labourers' – John Whitticombe (50), his son John Jnr (23) and Thomas Rowse (45) – living as far away as Tavistock. Clearly this was too far to commute daily, so these individuals would have taken lodgings nearby, their rent contributing to the local economy.

Before work commenced for the day, some form of 'signing in' would probably have taken place where workers were searched for tobacco, matches or any other smoking paraphernalia that may ignite the gunpowder.[14] This was a common practice in many powder factories and meant that employees, especially those who worked 'hands on' with gunpowder, had to be non-smokers or had to wait until after working hours to light up.[15]

The gunpowder factory covered a large area, where buildings were spread out in case one of them exploded. Within the walls of the main site there are the remains of at least eighteen buildings connected by numerous trackways and leats. Outside the factory perimeter was the manager's office, a forge, a cooperage for the production of barrels, and houses for many of its workers. There was also a magazine (gunpowder storehouse) located well away from the factory for obvious safety reasons. Tables 1 and 2 list the occupations of the workers in 1851 (the first census carried out at Powdermills) and shows how the production of gunpowder required the collaboration of skilled and unskilled people.

Table 1 Off-site Powdermill employees, 1851 (8 total)

Family name	Address	Age	Status within household	Occupation	Place of Birth
Bourne	Postbridge	35	Head	Powder labourer	Lydford
Hamlyn	Postbridge	29	Head	Powder labourer	Lydford
Coaker	Cherrybrook Bridge	49	Head	Gunpowder maker	Lydford
Hamlyn	Cherrybrook Bridge	25	Lodger	Gunpowder maker	Lydford

Cooper	Cherrybrook Bridge	27	Lodger	Labourer	Sth Tawton
King	Cherrybrook Bridge	23	Lodger	Cooper	Ashburton
Cleave	Cherrybrook Bridge	28	Lodger	Cooper	Chudleigh
Cook	Cherrybrook	25	Head	Cooper	Plymouth

Table 2 Occupations at Powdermills, 1851 (21 total)

Occupation	On site	Off site	Total
Gunpowder agent	1	0	1
Labourer	4	3	7
Cooper	5	3	8
Blacksmith	1	0	1
Miller	1	0	1
Gunpowder maker	1	2	3
Total	**13**	**8**	**21**

Everyone working with gunpowder had to live with the worry of it exploding, and each occupation had different risk factors. If the coopers, blacksmiths, wheelwrights, masons, carpenters, labourers and carters were working in their respective workshops or stables, clearly they were in less danger, but their job requirements often brought them into close contact with gunpowder (Table 2). The workers who actually produced the powder and the labourers who moved it around were in the greatest danger, as they spent large amounts of time working with the volatile substance. While most accidents occurred in the incorporating mills, it was the explosions in the corning and press houses that resulted in the greatest loss of life.[16]

It was standard practice throughout the gunpowder-making industry to use wood and copper tools to avoid making sparks. Workers also had to wear leather slippers over their footwear, and their trousers could not have pockets or turn-ups because these could carry grit which could get stuck in the works, and cause a spark.[17] In the mining industry similar precautions had to be taken when using gunpowder. A letter from mine employee William Grose, who worked at Hexworthy tin mine on Dartmoor *c*.1900, provides a description of the process involved in entering the mining company's powder magazine that was usually fenced off and locked:

On entering the first door there was a pair of large 'overshoes' that could be put on over the miner's working boots. These were made of thick leather and

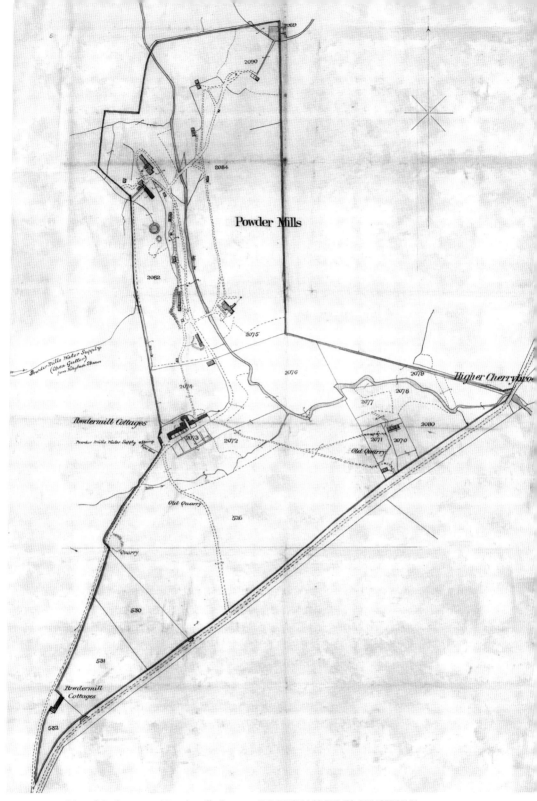

Map of the factory and Powdermills Cottages THE DUCHY ARCHIVES, PRINCETOWN

19

So what caused so many incidents in one year? It may have been because the previous year had seen numerous changes concerning the company's proprietors and the uncertainty at the 'top' may have in some way affected the workforce (Chapter 3). Then again it may have been simply bad luck. Very little is known about the workers who were killed; the press provides little information about them or the incidents, and does not bother to give the names of the first two victims in 1857. This is in stark contrast to the reporting of other accidents around the country which often provided graphic descriptions of the tragic events. It may simply have been a busy day for news, or perhaps the proprietors managed to limit the reporting through their connections as many of them (including the factory's founder, George Frean) were part owners in a company that published a local newspaper (see Chapter 2).[25] Research elsewhere can help to fill in the gaps. The censuses help us to calculate that at the time of Thomas Hamlyn's death he was thirty-six years old, married to Mary and with a daughter called Ann, aged five. The family did not live on-site and instead resided in nearby Postbridge. After her husband's death, Mary is recorded as taking on lodgers such as George Rowse aged twenty-two (in 1861), who was also employed at Powdermills as a labourer.[26]

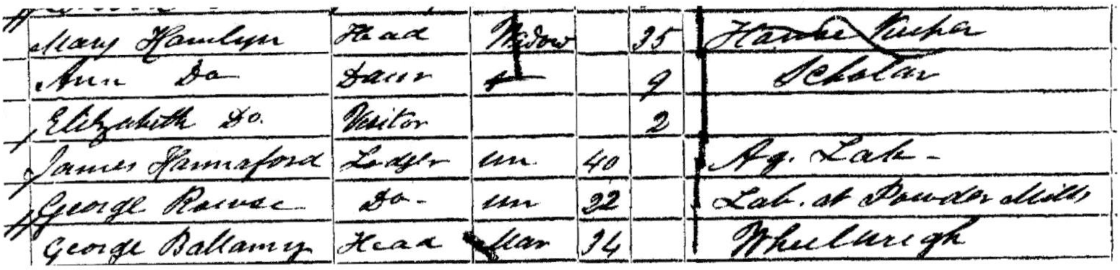

Mary Hamlyn	Head	Widow		35	[illegible]
Ann Do	Daur			9	Scholar
Elizabeth Do.	Visitor			2	
James Hannaford	Lodger	Un.	40		Ag. Lab.
George Rowse	Do.	Un	22		Lab. at Powder Mills
George Ballamy	Head	Mar	34		Wheelwright

Detail of the 1861 census listing the widow Mary Hamlyn and her lodger George Rowse
SOURCE T.N.A., RG 9/1458

Such violent and dramatic events often fuel folk tales and myths, and there is a long-established ghost story on Dartmoor of 'the giant hairy ape-like hands' which are supposed to belong to one of the workers killed in an explosion at the factory. They are said to appear at various locations on the road near the factory where they grope campers and cause accidents by forcing cyclists and motorists off the road. One source claims that the ghost was an Italian gunpowder worker who was infamous for having large hairy hands. The story goes that he inherited a large amount of money from a relative in Italy so decided to return home. On the night of his departure he had a leaving party and during the revelry realised he had left his tools in one of the working mills. He decided to retrieve them and when he entered the room a spark from hobnail boots caused an explosion leaving nothing of him but his hands![27]

Having survived a morning's work at the Powdermills, employees would break for lunch, with those living on-site perhaps going home for food and those living off-site having packed lunches. We have no records of the hours worked at the factory, but it is likely that they were reduced after 1874, when Parliament lowered the legal working hours from 60 to 56½. Without a minimum wage, this could equate to a direct and painful pay cut for many workers.[28]

Working with gunpowder was a dirty occupation: a report in 1861 portrays powder workers as having 'intensely black faces and lively eyes'.[29] Some works, such as the Fernilee Gunpowder Mills, provided washing facilities as described in the *High Peak News*:

> The back of the office has a neatly fitted up bath and wash house for the use of the begrimed workmen, who can thus, either with hot or cold water, cleanse themselves from the grimy substance by which they have become covered before returning to their homes.[30]

Some factories even had changing rooms for women, but that was not required on Dartmoor as there is no evidence of women working at the Powdermills.[31] As for toilet facilities, outside privies were uncommon until after 1875. Therefore, for the early years of the factory, it would have been a case of 'bucket and chuck it'.[32]

At the end of the working day

After work the employees of the factory made their way home to their families on- or off-site, or to their lodgings (providing they abstained from an early visit to the pub to quench their thirst). Derek Oddy explains how evening meals for the working class were any time between six and nine o'clock and the food eaten ranged from fish, meat or cheese dishes, 'all usually with potatoes', to meals that were 'made up of bread and tea alone'.[33]

The workers' evenings were either spent with their families or in pursuits away from home. Oddy adds that during this period:

Drinking to excess was widespread... beerhouses provided working men with space, warmth, light and an opportunity for a considerable range of social activities.[34]

We can get some idea of the sounds that could be heard from these establishments as William Crossing's *A Hundred Years on Dartmoor*, written in 1901, describes 'the speech of the peasant of the moor country is broad in the extreme, but there is a soft intonation of the voice which rather attracts', adding that the Dartmoor worker 'has a quiet humour, and his manner of relating a circumstance is often very quaint. Indeed, he is frequently unconsciously humorous'.[35] Drinking establishments also provided a place of 'refuge' from houses often overcrowded, as was possibly the case for the cooper Samuel White, who according to the 1881 census lived at Powdermills with his wife, eight children (including seven-week-old Charles) and his mother.

If on-site workers did decide to quench their thirst, it required a good walk as the nearest drinking establishment was the Saracen's Head Hotel (now the Two Bridges Hotel) at just under two miles, or just over two miles to the New Inn (now the East Dart Hotel), and of course they had to get back.[36] But for those who found working directly with the gunpowder stressful, and/or had a chaotic home, it was a price worth paying, even in bad weather.[37] It could have been much different:

When powder manufacture was at its height, and the workforce greatest in number, an application to build a public house near the site was submitted. George Frean was very much opposed to such a proposal, fearing it would result in drunkenness amongst the workforce. Negotiations resulted in him paying for improvements to an existing pub in nearby Postbridge, and the proposal for a new premises was dropped.[38]

In addition to drinking, wrestling was also a popular pursuit in the area. William Crossing describes how moor men were 'celebrated as players' because their hardiness enabled them to bear 'excessive kicking upon their shins', and he explains how at village revels, where there was 'a great amount of drinking... noise and excitement', the wrestlers' hats were decorated with winning ribbons for everyone to admire.[39] He also describes how the sport of cudgeling (stick fighting) was also popular with the moor men:

> Here the object to be attained by the player was the breaking of the opponent's head, the success of his praiseworthy efforts receiving the marked approval of the onlookers.[40]

Whether the evening was spent at home or at the pub, workers finally would have made their way to bed, knowing that they had provided once again for their families and survived another day working with or near gunpowder. However, it is possible that some workers were taking to their bed just as the household were waking, as at its height the factory was operating twenty-four hours and many workers were expected to put in a night shift. We know this because in 1849 the *Royal Cornwall Gazette* reported George Frean (Chapter 2) describing his gunpowder mills as being 'worked day and night and consequently one pair of stones could grind 240lbs a day'.[41] It is not known how frequent the practice of working nights was, but it must have been challenging, especially in the mill houses with no heating or light from a candle and fighting the need for sleep.

Once a week the workers received their pay. The amount they received would have been dependent on their position. Unfortunately no records have survived concerning the rates of pay for the workers at Powdermills, but in general gunpowder workers were paid extra due to the risks involved in their occupation. For example at the Schultze gunpowder factory in the New Forest gunpowder labourers were being paid £1 a week as opposed to local labourers employed elsewhere who were receiving 12 shillings.[42] For the employees of the Plymouth and Dartmoor Gunpowder Company, their jobs not only gave them a chance to earn 'danger money', it also provided them and their families with a regular income, camaraderie and the opportunity to live within a community that shared the risks and concerns.

CHAPTER 2
George Frean: the instigator

Mr George Frean of Plymouth, has long been an enthusiastic cultivator of the Moor and his straight forward character and practical sagacity are well known to all who come into contact with him.

West of England Conservative and Plymouth,
Devonport, and Stonehouse Advertiser 18 August, 1852

Now let's take a look at the life of the man whose name is synonymous with Dartmoor's gunpowder production. Mr Frean (as he was often referred to in the press) was the driving force behind establishing the gunpowder-making factory and worked tirelessly to promote numerous commercial ventures on and off the moor. In an age of social and economic possibility, men like George Frean transformed the political and industrial face of Britain, but he was arguably even more visionary than most.

George Frean's name recorded in the Castle Street Chapel Births and Baptisms 1793, Launceston, Cornwall SOURCE T.N.A., RG 4/428

Frean the businessman

George Frean was born on 2 September 1793 in Launceston, Cornwall, to Richard and Jane Frean, of whom little is known.[43] In 1816, aged twenty-three, George married Susan Moore (1797–1869) from Plymouth, who bore him in total eleven children.[44]

In Plymouth George prospered as a corn merchant and owner of mills.[45] As well as being successful in business he was also a resilient man, a trait that would serve him well in his Dartmoor enterprise. Despite some early setbacks – a legal dispute that nearly bankrupted him, and court proceedings involving his younger brother Richard – his business interests survived and prospered, so much so that he also invested in peat, railways, bone manure and cement.[46] Entrepreneurship ran in the family, and in 1857 his son George Henderson Frean formed (possibly under his father's stewardship) the pioneering biscuit company Peek Freans, and exported its produce across the empire.[47] The Frean family clearly had a talent for identifying opportunities in the expanding nineteenth-century marketplace and were not afraid to take risks, as exemplified by George's willingness to plough his money into starting a factory on Dartmoor making gunpowder: a notoriously volatile product.

George Frean Jnr; unfortunately no images of George Frean Snr have survived
SOURCE NEIL MATTINGLY

Frean the Dartmoor improver

Considering Plymouth's close proximity to Dartmoor it was perhaps unsurprising that George Frean's attention would turn to the commercial development of the moor. Phil Newman has described how during this period 'Dartmoor with open spaces and apparent abundant mineral and other resources attracted the attention of enthusiastic capitalists and adventurers searching for new ways to exploit it'.[48] Entrepreneurs and investors – such as Thomas Tyrwhitt in the Princetown area – set about enclosing large areas of land, increasing the output of the extractive industries, improving communications and promoting various forms of industrial activity on the moor.[49]

Following in Tyrwhitt's footsteps, by 1844 George Frean was leasing approximately 5000 acres of land on Dartmoor from the Crown. In a report delivered to the Duchy Council by its secretary, J.R. Gardiner, he recommends that Frean should be supported as he had 'zeal and enterprise' and that it was probable he would be granted a licence to build a gunpowder factory.[50] Gardiner's assumptions were correct, and in 1844 work began on the construction of a gunpowder-making factory.[51] A year later the following poem, written by someone only referring to themselves as 'H', was published in the *Western Times*:

To Mr Frean, on his patriotic attempt to conquer this waste for the use of men.

Amidst the relics of primeval time,
Amidst eternal durance and decay,
Where youngest things haden'd old and grey,
And rocks rear up their brows sublime,
Where seldom doth the lone way-farer climb –
The hand of God, a chronicle of old,
His character'd in ruins that in her prime,
The World may read. Yet thou whose purpose bold
Transform the desert to a dwelling place,
Go on: for firm as the Titan hold
What art my cover and old age deface,
Thou may at his limbs in garlands gaily dress,

Who for endowment of an unborn race
Dost win a garden from a wilderness.

Production began on Dartmoor in 1845. From the onset, the gunpowder was considered to be good quality and after a few years of operating, the

Statue of Prince Albert in Wolverhampton PHOTOGRAPH DAVID GRANGE

business had developed sufficiently to warrant the building of magazines (storehouses) in Exeter and Ashburton.[52] Possibly buoyed up by the early successes of the gunpowder factory, George decided in 1852 to contact Prince Albert to discuss how the development of Dartmoor could be furthered.[53] Queen Victoria's husband was renowned for his interest in such matters, and as Dartmoor was owned by the Royal Family, George was keen to encourage his involvement in future projects. Newspapers such as the *West of England Conservative and Plymouth, Devonport, and Stonehouse Advertiser*, reported the details of the discussions between the corn merchant and the prince and provide a wealth of information concerning George's passion for his work, his reputation and his predictions for Dartmoor's future:

> *18 August 1852*
>
> *Mr Frean had something on his mind for the good of Dartmoor, and the advancement of the temporal prosperity of the Duchy...*
>
> *Mr Frean was graciously received and attentively listened to...*
>
> *He told his Royal Highness what great things might be done for the Moor if the roads and draining were further carried out – how stout hearted projectors were talking of skirting the noble mountain region with the iron ways of the broad gauge...*
>
> *The Prince who likes Dartmoor, gave a patient hearing to suggestive ideas of the commoner, and when Mr Frean quitted, he was invited ...to go and see Prince Albert's farm.*

Frean the man

George's publicised meeting with Prince Albert must have greatly enhanced his reputation.[54] A year later he and his son had sufficient finances to buy the Manor of Charmouth, with its accompanying 'Langmoor House and 100 Acres of Meadowland' for £6500.[55] But despite being Lord of the Manor for Charmouth, George remained in Plymouth, presumably to be close to his business interests. The city's census returns indicate that George and his family lived a relatively modest existence in their Plymouth homes, as even with his mother, wife and ten children living with him in 1841, he employed only two servants (Table 3). Ten years later, still at Drakes Place, his mother is no longer there, and only six of his children are listed, with now only one servant and a visitor. By 1861, the family had moved to 3 Hill Park Crescent and downsized with George and his wife sharing their home with just their youngest daughter Susan and a servant.

CHARMOUTH.

takes its name from its position at the mouth of the river Chár, and is situated on the sea-coast. The living is a rectory, value £150, with residence. The incumbent is the Rev. Edward Breton, A.M. The church (St. Matthew) is a handsome flint and stone edifice, consists of nave, chancel, north and south aisles, and tower. There is an Independent chapel, well endowed; a National school, and an Independent school. George Frean, Esq., is lord of the manor. The population in 1861 was 678.

Extract from the Charmouth Directory, 1864 SOURCE NEIL MATTINGLY

Table 3 Census Returns, 1841 – The Frean family, Drakes Place, Plymouth, Devon

First name (s)	Last name	Gender	Age	Birth year	Birth place
Joan	Frean	Female	80	1761	
George	**Frean**	**Male**	**47**	**1794**	
George	Frean	Male	17	1824	Devon
Susan	Frean	Female	44	1797	Devon
Jane	Frean	Female	21	1820	Devon
Mary	Frean	Female	19	1822	Devon
Priscilla	Frean	Female	14	1827	
Elizabeth	Frean	Female	12	1829	
John	Frean	Male	10	1831	Devon
Thomas	Frean	Male	7	1834	Devon
Anna	Frean	Female	5	1836	Devon
Richard	Frean	Male	2	1839	Devon
Selina	Frean	Female	0	1841	Devon
Susan	Goddard	Female	20	1821	Devon
Betty	Freeble	Female	40	1801	Devon

It is said that George Frean was a considerate man, an opinion confirmed by a report in the *Woolmer's Exeter and Plymouth Gazette* of the evidence given by him against two men employed by Wombwell's Menagerie: George Field (alias Gypsy George) and George Chant. It reveals that Frean was a member of the Society for the Prevention of Cruelty to

Animals and he had followed Field, Chant and others into Barnstaple as he had been greatly distressed at their treatment of their horses.[56]

13 December 1851

Mr Frean said... he saw the two men together with others who had management of caravans... the horses had a great deal more to do than they ought to have had, they were in a miserable condition and the weight they had to draw was out of proportion to the strength they had...Chant had a powerful whip and lashed his horse unmercifully. Field was not so bad, but certainly his conduct was brutal.

George then described other atrocities carried out on these and other animals, and further informs the court that this was not an isolated incident: Wombwell's Menagerie had a history of abusing their animals and the society was determined to put a stop to these cruelties. Thanks to George's evidence both men were found guilty and the court fined the accused £1 each and sentenced them both to fourteen days in jail.

His concern for animals and his refusal to turn a blind eye to their harsh treatment indicates that George was a compassionate and courageous man; there is little 'bad press' concerning him. However, in the court case involving his brother Richard mentioned above – where George is accused of being a partner in his younger brother's failing milling business, and therefore required to pay its debts – a Baptist minister called Penrose is reported as stating that 'George Frean had villainously slandered him; and he was consequently severely cross-examined to show vindictive motive'.[57] Still, the overriding impression provided by contemporary newspapers is that George Frean was a respected man of good heart. He appears in the novel *Cherrybrook Rose*, which tells the fictitious story of Rose Maddiford (the daughter of the gunpowder factory manager). During a scene where George has to deliver bad news to Rose, we are given the following account:

His face had somehow sagged, and Rose was sure she could detect moisture in his concerned eyes. Mr Frean was a good man and always had been. A surrogate uncle, since she had no other relation but her father. She appreciated his integrity, his generosity in the circumstances.[58]

And in the Author's Note,

> George Frean was the real-life proprietor of the gunpowder mills. Research showed him to be a just and kindly gentleman, and he is portrayed thus in this novel.

George Frean worked tirelessly on behalf of the Plymouth and Dartmoor Gunpowder Company, but there is some uncertainty as to when he cut his ties with the business. On 28 October 1856 an article in the *Royal Cornwall Gazette* lists the proprietors of the company and George's name is not present.[59] Yet, it appears that he continued for some time to be involved with the business, as there is evidence of him writing to the Duchy land steward to arrange a meeting at the factory in 1866.[60] Perhaps – even though he was no longer a proprietor – he continued acting as a company manager.

Why George relinquished his part ownership in the company he started remains a mystery. He may have needed money for another venture, or maybe he realised that the company's fortunes were on the slide. He continued to be involved in developing Dartmoor, as revealed by a report in the *Western Times* of how George, now in his seventy-second year, was promoting a new venture:

> 10 November 1865
> Cattle Supply – George Frean invites the attention of the Capitalists...
> He is now prepared to provide for the use of a Joint Stock Company 6,000 Acres of Summer and Winter pasture at 20s an Acre, Land Tax included. The outlay will secure highly profitable returns at present prices in the Meat Market. Any persons willing to cooperate with him in forming this Company for the purpose are respectively requested to communicate with him George Frean, Endsleigh Villa, Plymouth.[61]

He also continued with his talks to learned societies on the subject of 'improvements' as the *Western Times* also reports:

> 23 September 1864
> George Frean of Plymouth read a paper in the Physiological section of Bath. The subject was on the use of Milk and Scottish Barley as an Article of Food.

The paper commanded respect by its practical and unpretentious character and led to an interesting discussion.

George Frean died in 1868 at the age of seventy-five.[62] Despite all his efforts, the moor did not develop into a utopia of cultivated fields and productive industry, where large numbers of settlements prospered and workers enjoyed full employment, happiness and health.[63] But off the moor, many of his business ventures were profitable and it could be considered that the gunpowder factory, for a period of time, was a success. In an article in the *Western Times* the reporter waxes lyrical about the 'extra strength' of the gunpowder and 'the absence of smoke', adding that it was so highly sought after that it 'has already induced the proprietors of important works in Wales, and the west and north of England, to enter into large contracts for its regular supply'.[64]

CHAPTER 3
The Plymouth and Dartmoor Gunpowder Company

The critical ingredient is getting off your butt and doing something. It's as simple as that. A lot of people have ideas, but there are few who decide to do something about them now. Not tomorrow. Not next week. But today. The true entrepreneur is a doer, not a dreamer.

Nolan Bushnell, entrepreneur

When George Frean had his 'eureka moment' regarding the idea of constructing a gunpowder factory on Dartmoor, several factors may have helped him in terms of its commercial potential:

• There was a thriving extraction industry (quarrying and mining) on Dartmoor that needed gunpowder.

• Farmers on the moor could benefit from using gunpowder to remove large rocks off their fields.

• The nearest competition was from the Kennall Gunpowder factory in Ponsanooth, Cornwall, some 70 miles away.[65]

• The land around Cherry Brook was of poor quality and therefore cheap to rent. Producing gunpowder was risky and to minimise the damage from explosions each process had to be carried out in separate buildings positioned a significant distance from each other.

• The proposed factory could be situated away from major settlements (for safety reasons).

• There was water from the Cherry Brook to provide power for the mills.

• There was an abundance of granite for building material.

• The site was close to a turnpike road which led off the moor.

The construction of Powdermills

Having found what seemed to be the perfect location for their factory, George and his associates had to apply to the county courts for a licence to produce gunpowder. An article in the *Oxford University, City and County Herald* in November 1844 reports:

Gunpowder – Permission has been granted to Messrs Frean and Co, of Plymouth to erect a set of powder-mills on Dartmoor. The mills will be erected on the Cherry Brook Estate and will be extensive. The site selected is ten miles from Mortenhamstead and two miles from Two Bridges. The nearest point of the mill to the turnpike road is 728 yards of three feet each. The nearest point of the magazine to the road is 520 yards. The distance between the mills and the magazine will be 1,200 yards.[66]

One of the mills built following the issue of the second licence

With the licence issued, George gave instructions to begin construction in the winter of 1844/5: not the best time of year to start a building project, especially on Dartmoor! However, the weather turned out to be the least of his problems, as it became apparent that the Cherry Brook would not provide sufficient water to drive the numerous waterwheels that were being built on its west bank. This must have been a serious blow to Frean and his supporters, not to mention the builders out there battling

William Henry Hodge, John Wakeham Sparrow, Benjamin Sparrow, John Burnell, James Bryant and William Eales were involved in financing both the newspaper and the gunpowder factory.[79] Clearly these gentlemen speculators, many of whom lived in Plymouth, operated within a local network, where information was shared concerning so called 'good prospects' and it is probable that through their joint involvement in other companies, vestries, charities, campaign groups and county courts, there would have been a degree of familiarity between them.[80]

Table 4 Initial Investors in the Plymouth and Dartmoor Gunpowder Company

Name	Status	Place of Residence	Changes to the partnership in 1846
James Bryant	Gentleman	Plymouth, Devon	Sold his shares
William Henry Hodge	Gentleman	Plymouth, Devon	Sold his shares
William Burnell	Gentleman	Plymouth, Devon	Sold his shares
John Burnell	Gentleman	Plymouth, Devon	Sold his shares
John Wakeham Sparrow	Gentleman	Plymouth, Devon	
Benjamin Sparrow Junr	Gentleman	Plymouth, Devon	
John Coulson	Miller	Penzance, Cornwall	
William Eales	Merchant	London	
William Polkinhorn	Miller	Gwennap, Cornwall	Sold his shares
Peter Adams	Draper	Plymouth, Devon	Purchased more shares
Joseph Nicholas Bennett	Solicitor	Plymouth, Devon	Purchased more shares
George Frean	Miller	Plymouth, Devon	Purchased more shares
Joseph Blake Triscott	Accountant	Plymouth, Devon	
Thomas Baron Tyeth	Accountant	Plymouth, Devon	Purchased more shares
Thomas Tregaskis	Gentleman	Perran Wharf, Cornwall	
John Tregaskis	Gentleman	Perran Wharf, Cornwall	
Thomas Eales Soady		East Stonehouse, Devon	

A year on from the company's formation newspapers such as the *London Gazette* reported that five of the seventeen investors were selling their shares to four of the partners (Table 4). Clearly they were unhappy with some aspect of the company's operation or future prospects.[81] Nevertheless, the fact that a group of the partners, including Frean, were prepared to plough more money into the venture indicates their commitment and faith in the company.

foreign trade', yet 'at least one third of the present proprietary would, if desired, unite with the purchaser to carry on an extended business'.[85]

The company was in trouble – its local market had dwindled and there was clearly much disagreement between its partners. Its saviour, albeit temporarily, came in the form of Charles Francis Williams as revealed by the *London Gazette*:

> *10 November 1871*
>
> *NOTICE is; hereby given, that the Partnership lately existing between us the undersigned, except Mr. Charles Francis Williams, carrying on business under the style and firm of the Plymouth and Dartmoor Gunpowder Company, has been dissolved, and that the said business is henceforth intended to be carried on under the same style and firm by the said Charles Francis Williams. — Dated this 28th day of September, 1871.*

The partnership was to be dissolved again, allowing one of the owners, Charles Francis Williams, to become its sole proprietor. Williams owned timber mills in Plympton and supplied the gunpowder works, which may be why he bought the business.[86] Charles kept his timber company operating while owning the Powdermills as revealed by the 1861 census where he is described as 'a timber merchant employing 30 men' and in 1871 he is listed as a 'timber merchant, green grocer, manufacturer' (Table 5). Charles Francis Williams Snr appeared to have little involvement in the running of the company and instead relied on his son and nephew to take care of things:

> *He turned to Robert Chaff who he appointed day-to-day manager and his son Charles Francis who appears to have had control over the money.*[87]

Table 5 Census Returns, 1871 – Charles Williams, Glenfield House, Plympton St Mary

Charles F. Williams	73	Head	Timber merchant, greengrocer and manufacturer	Devon
Maria Williams	73	Wife		Cornwall
Henrietta Spur	35	Visitor		Devon
Sarah Ward	40	Servant		Devon

After ten years of owning the company, Charles Francis Williams Snr died in 1881 leaving his assets, including the powder mill, to his son Charles Jnr, described in the 1871 census as a ship builder from Plympton St Mary. With the 'boss's son' in charge the company's fortunes continued to decline, due mainly to a slump in the Dartmoor extractive industries and the fact that safer chemical explosives such as dynamite were being used instead of gunpowder.[88] Following a steady reduction in the workforce the company was finally wound up in 1897.

In conclusion

Analysis of the ownership of the Plymouth and Dartmoor Gunpowder Company reveals that initially it was one man, George Frean, who promoted the venture, but as the idea turned into a reality he opted to turn the company into a partnership. The reports of the dissolving of these partnerships provide snapshots of the investors in the company and reveals how during this period at least thirty-one people were partners in the business. Three of them – Peter Adams, John Nicholas Bennett and Thomas Baron Tyeth – are listed as owners from the start of the company until its take-over by the Williams family in 1871 (Table 6).[89]

It is not known how involved these partners were in the decision-making process. For most of the years the company traded its offices were in Plymouth, so it is possible that many of the owners had little, if anything, to do with the day-to-day running of the factory and rarely ventured on Dartmoor to visit the factory.[90] By the end of the 1860s it would appear that most of the company's partners no longer believed in the commercial viability of the company, leaving the fortunes of the business to the Williams family who, despite running the business for over twenty years, failed to prevent the factory's inevitable closure.

Table 6 Partners in the Company up until 1871

Name	1847	1854	1856	1871
William Burnell	*			
James Bryant	*			
John Burnell	*			
John Wakeham Sparrow	*			
William Henry Hodge	*			
Benjamin Sparrow (jnr.)	*			
John Coulson	*			
William Eales	*			
William Polkinhorn,	*			
Peter Adams	*	*	*	*
John Nicholas Bennett	*	*	*	*
George Frean	*	*		
Joseph Blake Triscott	*			
Thomas Baron Tyeth	*	*	*	*
Thomas Tregaskis	*	*	*	
John Tregaskis	*			
Thomas Eales Soady	*	*	*	
James Dabb		*	*	
Edward Crispe Ellery		*	*	*
Samuel Picken		*	*	*
Eliana Soper		*	*	
Robert Barclay Fox		*		
Henry Luscombe		*		
Jane Gurney Fox			*	
Charles Francis Williams				*
Richard Rundle				*
James B. Wilcocks				*
Henry Brown				*
William Symons				*
Thomas S. Sutton				*
A.C. Hope				*

* represents their names being listed

CHAPTER 4
The workers and their families

They built the houses on what could only be described as croutons in a bowl of soup.

Joss Hibbs explaining how, despite the boggy land at Powdermills, the builders managed to find some hard ground for constructing the workers' homes, 2017

The Dartmoor gunpowder factory employed both local residents and 'outsiders' from other areas, many of whom moved with their families to live in the factory grounds. Census returns, marriage registers and local newspaper reports from the time help us to understand more about the numbers involved, the jobs they did and the dynamics of the workers' families, and give occasional insights into certain events that affected and shaped people's lives at Powdermills.

Family life

The factory's isolated location meant that in 1845 the local population was insufficient to fill all the available posts. Consequently the Plymouth and Dartmoor Gunpowder Company encouraged workers from outside Lydford (the parish in which the factory was located) to move to the area and live on-site. The workers' accommodation included houses on the same row as the blacksmith's forge and the cooperage (Powdermill Cottages), cottages

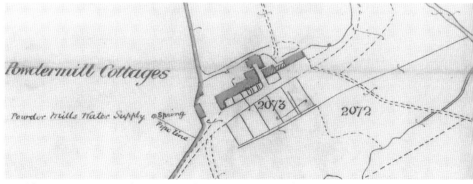

Detail from an undated map of the Powdermills site, showing some of the workers' accommodation
THE DUCHY ARCHIVES, PRINCETOWN

close to the magazine (also Powdermill Cottages) and probably houses close to Higher Cherrybrook Bridge, which may have been called Sunnyside Cottages.[91] Only the former of these have survived, with the others now in ruins (see Chapter 1). The detailed map extract on the previous page shows how the Powdermill Cottages had what looks like garden plots, which would have provided a much-needed source of fresh vegetables.

The first census to record the Powdermills' residents was taken in 1851 (Table 7). The factory had been in operation for six years and had seven households, where labourers, craftsmen and management lived side by side, along with their wives, twenty-six children and eleven lodgers. In one house lived the gunpowder agent James Lobb (who later became the works' manager: see Chapter 5), his wife Charity and Elizabeth Martin, who was either a servant or family friend. As they were yet to have children and did not have lodgers (unlike many of the other households), it can be assumed that this was one of the quieter residences. Next door would have been a different tale as there lived the labourer Robert Northcott, his wife Elizabeth and their seven children aged between one and fifteen. The Northcotts still found room for a lodger named Joseph Smith, who was employed as a cooper. The Northcotts' was not the only household with occupants in double figures as the miller Thomas Daw and his wife Elizabeth also had a household of ten, with five children and three lodgers crammed under one roof.

Table 7 Powdermills residents, 1851 (51 total)

Family name	Age of husband and wife	Number of workers' children	Number of lodgers/non family	Occupation of head of family	From Devon	From Cornwall
Lobb[92]	39/36	0	1	Gunpowder agent	2	1
Northcott	40/40	7	1	Labourer	10	0
Hexter	39/37	5	0	Blacksmith	7	0
Cornell	31/31	2	2	Cooper	6	0
Daw	28/33	5	3	Miller	10	0
Hall	37/55	3	3	Not given	7	1
Martin	43/40	4	1	Gunpowder maker	0	7

So where did all these people come from? With one exception, none of the workers, their wives or children over five years old were born in Lydford. Research has shown that during this period it was common for people to move away from their 'birth parish' and that 'in 1851, 54 percent of the population were recorded as not living within two

Powdermill Cottages today. The manager's house with the large porch is positioned centre right with workers' cottages (far left) and the cooperage (right) ILLUSTRATION PENNY CAMPBELL

kilometres of their stated place of birth'.[93] Within the Powdermills community of 1851, the only people registered as being born in Lydford were a man named Mathew who lodged with the Daw family and the children of the Northcotts, Hexters and the Daws, who were all under five years of age. Ann Hall possibly holds the distinction of being the first child born at the works. All children over the age of five are registered as being born outside the area, supporting the notion that these families relocated to the gunpowder factory.

Brought together for the financial necessity of employment, this was a community of 'outsiders' (with a large contingent from Cornwall) facing the challenge of living and working in a new area, with people they had probably never met before.[94] While the available sources provide their names, age, sex, occupation and place of origin, occasionally more personal aspects of their lives come to light. For example, the 1851 census lists the works' manager James Martin (see Chapter 5 – in the returns he is listed as a gunpowder maker), living with his wife Maryann and their four children – the eldest being nineteen-year-old Catherine. The family originated from Cornwall and took on a fellow Cornishman as a lodger, twenty-four-year-old Francis Paddy, who was employed as a cooper (barrel-maker). Interestingly, the marriage records of the same year reveal that living with his manager's family did not deter Francis from becoming involved with his boss's daughter, as on 11 August 1851 he and Catherine were married. We will probably never know whether the union had the family's blessing or not, but a romance between the factory manager's daughter and an employee who was living under the same roof would have at least been a talking point for both the workers and their families.[95]

Ten years down the line, the census for 1861 records massive changes to the community at Powdermills (Table 8). Not only had the number of households increased from seven to fourteen but, with the exception of the Lobbs (James was now the works' manager) and the Ash family,[96] most of the local workforce had changed.[97] Being dismissed, retiring or moving on in search of better prospects were all common occurrences, but it is difficult to understand why so many people left their jobs and homes, especially as these families had moved to the area specifically to work in the factory.[98] Perhaps the deaths and injuries during 1851 and 1857 were too much for some people, and for the sake of their safety and financial security they opted to leave. Maybe some were sacked because of the incidents, or changes at the 'top' prompted people to leave. Once again the company chose to bring in 'outsiders' as, with the exception of one (the labourer Jeffrey Eden), all the residential workers and their wives were from parishes other than Lydford, with William Baron from Kent and Edwin Wicks from as far away as Jersey.

Table 8 Powdermills residents, 1861 (89 total)

Family name	Age of husband and wife	Number of workers' children	Number of Lodgers	Occupation of head of family	From Devon	Other Counties
Bellamy	34/34	5	2	Wheelwright	9	0
Milliman	40/29	3	3	Carpenter	8	0
Lannaford	26/24	4	0	Employed at Powder Mill	5	1 (Cornwall)
King	33/35	5	0	Cooper	7	0
Lobb	48/45	3	0	Manager	4	1 (Cornwall)
Tribble	25/25	2	0	Labourer	4	0
Ash	32/39	4	0	Carter	6	0
Frick	32/33	3	1	Blacksmith	6	0
Stone	34/36	3	2	Not given	6	1 (Kent)
Mortimore	25/33	1	0	Carpenter	3	0
The school						
Cornish	37/32	5	1	Waggoner	6	2 (Cornwall)
Casher	37/35	6	2	Waggoner	10	0
Eden	24/24	2	1	Labourer	4	1 (Jersey)
James	56/57	2	1	Labourer	2	3 (Cornwall)

The 1860s has controversially been described as the best decade in English history in which to be raised.[99] Whether or not the residents of Powdermills would have agreed is debatable; what we do know is that fourteen families with forty-eight children lived on site in 1861 (Table

The Powdermills workers' cottages and service buildings; the building far left is the current-day Powdermills Gallery, probably the works' school

8), prompting the company to build a school (most likely the present-day pottery gallery), which is also listed in the census (Table 8). The company had no legal obligation to provide an education for the workers' children as it was not until 1880 that the government made education compulsory for children under the age of ten. At Powdermills it was probably the best way to control and monitor a large group of children, while the workforce got on with producing gunpowder. It is also possible that this building doubled up as a chapel, as in 1907, ten years after the factory closed, fire insurance was taken out on the buildings that were in use with one listed as Chapel Stable and described as being detached.[100]

Raising children at Powdermills would have brought many challenges. The weather would have kept them indoors for large periods of time (nearby Princetown has twice the amount of rain as Plymouth). It is often said of Dartmoor that it has 'nine months winter and three months bad weather'.[101] Observing the properties today it is clear that space would have been tight, especially in households with large families and lodgers. Also, many areas would have been out of bounds. Parents must have had concerns about raising their children in such a potentially dangerous environment, especially with the factory sometimes operating twenty-four hours a day.

The youngest recorded employees were fifteen-year-old Samuel

White who lived in Postbridge in 1861, and Frederick King who lived at Powdermills in 1871. There were also three sixteen-year-olds employed as coopers in 1861: John Bell and Frederick Pulleyblank (who lodged with a family at Powdermills) and Richard French who lived in Postbridge. It appears the factory's young employees were first taught to make barrels in the cooperage, where it was safer, as there are no records of any workers under twenty-one doing other jobs.[102] Presumably it was considered too risky to have young and inexperienced men in close contact with gunpowder. The cooperage must have been a busy place:

> Barrels were usually made of oak and often clad with leather to stop spillage. Most gunpowder factories had their own cooperage and employed their own coopers. The number of tradesmen engaged in this occupation at the Dartmoor works would have accounted for around 20 percent of the workforce.[103]

The works' cooperage

There are no records of any women working for the company, and of the thirty-five female adults listed in the 1851–91 returns only three women – Charlotte Ash, Elizabeth Mortimer and Susan Bellamy – are described as having an occupation, all of them being dressmakers. The national average for females in employment at this time (1851–81) was 26 percent, therefore the Powdermills' women were well below average.[104] It is probable that the low employment rate for these female residents was due to the factory's isolated position. Some of the families' daughters in their mid- to late teens may have left home and found employment in service, because there were no other opportunities in the area for work. This notion is supported by the fact that over five decades only three females aged 16–20 are recorded as living with their families on site.

All homes operate differently, and the residents of Powdermills were no exception. Factors affecting their success as a family unit would have included money (or lack of it), the numbers of children and lodgers living under their roof, and the temperament and personalities of the people within the household. Within the marriage contract men and women had defined roles when it came to work and looking after the house; working men during this period provided financial support 'in return for wives household management, cooking and sexual services'.[105]

A married man was expected to turn out all housekeeping and childcare over to his wife when he turned over ('tipped up') his weekly wage. Customs varied between industries and area as to what proportion the husband kept for himself but basic principles were similar... [wives] ...prided themselves in their ability to keep the household at the highest standards according to neighbourhood norms. When families were large and the burden of care so great there was little time and energy left for demonstrations of affection to children. Devotion had to be expressed in the fierce attention to cleanliness and behaviour, which made many mothers seem harsh and joyless... A good husband was one who contributed regular and when possible, sufficient support and was not violent particularly towards the children... Many men did help with housework or childcare but they risked being dubbed 'mop rag' or 'diddy man'... Husbands expected their comforts to be considered, to have their meals ready as much to their taste as possible. A wife who was not able or did not bother to keep up these standards was demonstrably not living up to her part of the marriage contract.[106]

The next census taken for 1871 reveals that people were staying at Powdermills longer, as out of thirteen families listed over half had been there for more than ten years (Table 9). There are also fascinating details concerning some of the households. John Milliman, who was from Hatherleigh, and his wife Mary lived with their six children, including nine-month-old twins Clara and Emily; William Cornish and his wife Mary from Milton Abbot were raising seven children aged between six months and eighteen years, with the oldest, William Jnr, described as being 'disabled with polio'. None of the households in 1871 had a lodger living with them (Table 9), whereas the previous census recorded thirteen throughout eight families. Lodgers have been described as the 'shadowiest of all the social groups', and by 1851 'were present in 12 percent of all households'.[107] The lodgers living with the factory families in 1851 and 1861 were all employed by the company and most were young, single males, but by 1871 they had all left. Perhaps the Powdermills families were doing so well that they did not need the extra money from renting out a room. Maybe the company's fortunes were dipping and the first employees to lose their jobs would have been lodgers. Company profits may have been falling, but the production of children did not, as the returns for 1871 list fifty-two children, the highest recorded in the community's history.

Six years after the 1871 census was taken, some of the Powdermills residents were involved in a court case concerning an alleged assault. In October 1877 the *Western Times* provided the following report made by the prosecution:

On the 25th June, Jane James was returning from Princetown to her new house (at the Powdermill) between 9 and 10 pm, in company with a little girl, when the prisoner (James Parr) overtook them and commenced chatting on various subjects. After they had walked some distance he suddenly confronted her in an indecent manner and attempted to criminally assault her. She shouted murder and the man endeavoured to stifle her cries.[108]

Census returns for 1871, showing the Cornish family SOURCE T.N.A., RG 10/2144

The report continues to describe how the little girl ran back to Princetown for help which arrived in time to find Jane alive, but her attacker had disappeared. Parr was later found in a drunken state near his home at Rundlestone, coming from the direction of the alleged assault. Jane James (possibly fearing for her own safety) claimed she could not say for sure if it was Parr who carried out the assault as it was dark at the time, but the little girl swore in court that Parr was her attacker.

The court case continued into the New Year and Emily Williams (the Powdermills manager's daughter) and William Bellamy (a waggoner employed by the factory) were called to give evidence as the courting couple had witnessed the attack while out on a walk. However, under cross examination neither of them could be positive that it was James Parr who had committed the crime – again giving the failing light as a reason. As the little girl (who remained unnamed) was the only witness who would testify against him, James Parr, who had relatives in Postbridge also employed at the factory, was found not guilty.[109]

Table 9 Powdermills residents, 1871 (78 total)

Family name	Age of husband and wife	Number of workers' children	Lodgers or relatives (R)	Occupation of head of family	From Devon	Other Counties
James	64/42	2	0	Gunpowder maker	1	3 (Cornwall)
Slee	40/39	5	0	Powder maker	7	0
Tuckett	27/21	1	0	Waggoner	3	0
Cornish	47/41	7	0	Waggoner	9	0
Martin	63/63	1	0	Miller	3	0
Stone	44/46	2	0	Mason	3	1 (Guernsey)
King	42/43	7	0	Cooper	9	0
Ash	42/43	4	0	Powder maker	6	0
Milliman	56/38	6	0	Carpenter	8	0
Eden	34/34	3	1 (R)	Cooper	5	1 (Cornwall)
Smith	38/31	5	0	Agricultural Labourer	5	2 (Cornwall)
Mouse	0/32	4	0		5	0
Bellamy	44/44	5	0	Wheelwright	7	0

Three years on from the court case, the 1881 census reflects the company's woeful fortunes (Table 10). The community is described as seven families of thirty-seven people of whom twenty-three were either children or grandchildren. The workforce size had plummeted to the extent that the company were not employing anyone unless they lived on-site.

Robert Williams SOURCE DR STEVE CHILDS

It was also a sad time in the household of the works' manager Robert Williams; following the marriage of his daughter Emily to William Bellamy (another member of the workforce marrying the manager's daughter), Emily died aged twenty-seven, quite possibly as a result of giving birth to their second child. She left behind William Bellamy aged one, Charles Bellamy aged one month, and their father William Bellamy Snr, who are listed as living with his in-laws (Table 11). Charles Francis Bellamy went on to start his own family in Princetown where he was employed as a 'driver at hotel'. Following service in World War I, Charles died as a result of his wounds.[110] He and his mother Emily are buried together in the churchyard at Princetown.

The graves of Emily Jane Bellamy and her son Charles Francis at the church of St Michael and All Angels, Princetown PHOTOGRAPHS RODERICK MARTIN

Table 10 Powdermills residents, 1881 (37 total)

Family name	Age of husband and wife	Number of workers' children	Lodgers, relatives	Occupation of head of family	From Devon	Other Counties
Slee	50/0	2	0	Powder Maker	3	0
White	35/32	7	1 (Mother)	Cooper	8	2 (Cornwall and Wilts)
Milliman	0/47	1	0	Mother (sick)	1	1 (Cornwall)
Bickell	31/30	1	0	Cooper	3	0
Lance	38/46	2	0	Powder Maker	4	0
Bellamy	54/54	1	0	Cooper	3	0
Williams	53/52	7	3 (1 son-in-law, 2 grandchildren)	Manager	12	0

Table 11 Details from the 1881 census

Robert Williams	53	Head	Manager of Powdermills	Plymouth, Devon
Mary J.	52	Wife		Yealmpton, Devon
Frederick J.	29	Son	Carpenter	Ermington, Devon
Louisa B.	25	Daughter		Ermington, Devon

Edmund M.	22	Son	Carpenter	Ermington, Devon
Robert C.	18	Son	Carpenter	Ermington, Devon
George R.H.	15	Son	Scholar	Ermington, Devon
Sydney F.	12	Son	Scholar	Ermington, Devon
Ernest A.	8	Son	Scholar	Lydford, Devon
William H. Bellamy	26	Son in law	Wagoner	Lydford, Devon
William F.G. Bellamy	1	Grandson		Lydford, Devon
Charles F. Bellamy	1m	Grandson		Lydford, Devon

The census of 1891 records five families living at Powdermills, of which three (all Bellamys) were related to each other (Table 12). Thirty years before, this once-thriving community included over fifty children, but by 1891 the numbers were down to six.

Table 12 Powdermills residents, 1891 (17 total)

Family name	Age of husband and wife	Number of children	Lodgers or relatives	Occupation of head of family	From Devon	Other Counties
Bellamy	22/23	2	0	Cooper	4	0
Bellamy	62/60	0	1 (Grandson)		3	0
Bellamy	26/26	0	0	Wheelwright/Smith	2	0
French	32/33	0	1 (Mother)		3	0
Williams	0/39	3	1 (Tutor)	Wife of manager	4	0

There are few surviving pictures of people employed at or involved with the factory, but there is one of Jonas Coaker, born at Hartland, Postbridge. The much-written-about 'Dartmoor Poet' (whose work includes *Dartmeet*) and one-time landlord of what is now the Warren House Inn was employed at the factory during its early years as in 1851 he was recorded as a 'Gunpowder Maker' living in Postbridge.[111] In addition to his wages, he made money by providing accommodation for three gunpowder factory employees and one of their wives, who are all recorded as lodgers. We are not sure how long he lasted as an employee, but by 1861 he is recorded living in the nearby Cherrybrook Farm where he is described as a farmer of twenty-five acres.[112]

Jonas Coaker (1801–90) SOURCE WILLIAM WRIGHT[114]

Dartmeet

A maiden fair from the West came down
Clad in a dress of the brightest brown;
'Twas trimmed all o'er with silv'ry frill,
Spangled with white, like rippling rill,
If you gazed into her crystal eye,
With a liquid glance she passed you by,
Bounding and dancing with skippings fleet
Swift as Dart her lover to meet.

A dashing youth from the East drew nigh,
Dark grey was his suit, bright brown was his eye;
His buttons were silver, sparkling bright,
The lining silk, of a glossy white,
If stared at long, or gazed by chance;
'Twas ever the same unflinching glance;
With a leaping, bounding, merry Dart,
He tried to meet but his own sweetheart.

It was here they met one wintry morn,
Never again were their lives forlorn;
No priest was required to make them one,
For their wedding day was known to none;
The stream of their lives right merrily sped,
Together they roamed where Nature led;
Their will was one, their purpose alone
In the sea of Love to lose their own.[113]

A fluctuating population

In the mid-1960s the writer Helen Harris met with Mr R.G. Stephens and his wife who had lived and farmed at Powdermills for many years. Recounting her visit and writing in 2016, Helen describes how Mr Stephens had been told by many locals that around a hundred people were employed by the company:

> I visited him in the summer of 1965 and I remember, after I had had a good look around, we sat on granite rocks and he told me all about the industry there, in which the fathers of both himself and his wife had worked. The employment of 100 people seems astonishing today, and it is possible that there was a degree of generalising or slight exaggeration in the numbers local people were quoting. There were various ancillary activities which would take account of some, and I think that at times there would have been quite a bit of casual as well as regular employment. They may not have all been working at the same time. Much depended on the ups and downs of the neighbouring mines, and work would often be found for those laid off, in maintenance jobs – cleaning out the leat, repairing the tracks etc.

So did the factory really employ 100 people, or might the figure have been exaggerated over the years? Detailed examination of the census returns for the whole of Dartmoor (1851–91) reveal that the numbers employed were much lower; the returns for 1861 listed the greatest number of people who can be positively described as employees of the company and this figure came to thirty-six (Table 13). There were others employed by the company, such as those working in the numerous magazines (storehouses) – many of which were located on the outskirts of the moor – and there would have also have been some people working in the offices in Plymouth. It is also possible that some Dartmoor labourers/craftsmen may have put down their occupation without specifying they were employed by the gunpowder factory and therefore are not included in this calculation, and some people would have been employed part-time or even seasonally. Even taking these factors into account, there would not have been sufficient numbers to make the difference up to 100.[115]

However, looking at the number of people who were living on-site changes the picture. The figure below shows the numbers of people living at Powdermills recorded in ten-yearly intervals and reveals how the community's population was at its highest in 1861 at eighty-nine. Yet it also shows that a large proportion of these residents were the

Population of the Dartmoor Powdermills taken from 1851–91 Census

workers' children and wives.[116] Nevertheless, adding the number of the 1861 residents to the twelve employees listed as living off-site (Table 13) gives a figure of 101. Therefore it's fair to say that at its peak (in 1861) the factory had over a hundred residents and employees.

Table 13 Occupations of Powdermills employees, 1861 (36 total)

Occupations	On-site	Off-site	Total
Labourer	7	9	16
Carpenter	2	0	2
Cooper	6	3	9
Employed at Powdermills	2	0	2
Blacksmith (Journeyman)	1	0	1
Manager	1	0	1
Powder maker	1	0	1
Carter/Waggoner	3	0	3
Wheelwright	1	0	1
Total	**24**	**12**	**36**

The rise and fall in numbers of workers and residents is mirrored in the fortunes of the company. By 1851 a considerable workforce and community had been established and by 1861, despite a number of accidents/fatalities, the business was clearly doing well and expanding. Ten years on (and despite a small drop in residents/workers) the company was still in good shape, but by 1881 it is clear that the business was struggling as the number of employees/residents fell noticeably. By 1891 the Plymouth and Dartmoor Gunpowder Company was clearly on its last legs as only seventeen people are recorded as living at Powdermills, with a total workforce of four men (Table 14).

Table 14 Employees of Powdermills, 1891 (4 total)

Occupations	On-site	Off-site	Total
Powder makers	2	1	3
Wheelwright and Smith	1	0	1
Total	**3**	**1**	**4**

People still live and work at Powdermills today, in the homes that once belonged to the workers at the gunpowder factory. But the numbers are much smaller and their occupations less dangerous. Joss and Martin Hibbs moved from London in 1999 and have raised two children in this unique environment. Joss makes wood-fired tableware which she sells, along with the works of other local potters, artists and musicians, at their Powdermills Gallery. Martin, in addition to working in the shop and café, is also employed by Spirit of Adventure which provides adventure holidays. Both 'incomers' say they are grateful for the fact that everyone gets on within their small community. 'We're lucky having a car,' says Martin, 'I injured my leg and couldn't drive for months – so I've some idea of how the workers may have felt trapped living here'. Joss adds 'We're so isolated – it's almost like living on an island. Plus the weather can be a challenge, as we get more rain, stronger winds and colder temperatures, than places off the moor.' But for this family there are more positives than negatives. 'While the kids didn't have any friends living nearby they had the freedom to roam free, and once they learnt to ride hill ponies they would meet up with other children who lived on the moor and all ride from one ice cream van to another.' Joss further describes how the landscape constantly amazes and inspires her: 'I'm sure the kids will appreciate it a lot more when they leave, but sometimes I don't think they see what we're seeing. We once had an amazing sunset and I asked them to draw what they saw outside. So they drew pictures of our car.'

CHAPTER 5
Running the gunpowder factory

The world is not fair, and often fools, cowards, liars and the selfish hide in high places.
Bryant H. McGill, writer, speaker and activist

Manufacturing companies need more than just 'good owners' and 'good men on the ground'. The Plymouth and Dartmoor Gunpowder Company needed factory managers who were honest, diplomatic, respected and prepared to live on-site with their families. It also needed to transport its produce and raw materials and build, in specific locations, magazines for storing the gunpowder. Furthermore, it had to employ agents to drum up sales, take orders and ensure that customers got what they paid for – and no more than they paid for!

James Martin

James Martin was the first manager of the factory. The 1851 census lists him at 'Powder Mill W' with his wife Maryann and four children (Table 15). Like many of the factory's employees, James and his family were from Cornwall, and had moved to Dartmoor to work at the factory.

Table 15 James Martin, Powder Mill W, 1851

James Martin	Head	43	Gunpowder Maker	Cornwall
Maryann	Wife	40		Cornwall
Catherine	Daughter	19		Cornwall
James	Son	14		Cornwall
Maryann	Daughter	12		Cornwall
Jane	Son	10		Cornwall
Francis Paddy	Lodger	24	Cooper	Cornwall, Mylor

Considerable money and time were invested in building the gunpowder mills, and James would have been under enormous pressure from owners and employees to deal with the teething problems that must have occurred during the early stages of production. Managing the works would have been no easy task. James had to ensure the factory worked to its maximum capacity, placate factory inspectors who could turn up at any time, oversee the safety of the workers and keep an eye on the new settlement of workers, many of whom were from Cornwall. There are no records detailing James' earnings, but the fact that the family took on a lodger, Francis Paddy (who became his son-in-law), suggests that the company did not have sufficient accommodation for its workforce and that the Martin family needed the extra money.

After approximately six years, James Martin was replaced by his brother-in-law James Lobb as manager of the factory. The circumstances of his departure are not known, but he returned to Cornwall and carried on working in the gunpowder industry.[117]

The home of James Martin and subsequent works' managers

James Lobb

James Lobb (also from Cornwall) was already employed by the company as a gunpowder agent.[118] James grew up near the Cornish gunpowder factories at Ponsanooth. His brother Henry progressed from being a powder labourer to managing a gunpowder-making plant at Herodsfoot in Cornwall where he held a one-sixth share of the company. His older brother, William, travelled extensively around South and North America collecting plants and is credited as introducing to Britain the monkey puzzle tree. He also brought back the recipe for the more efficient Peruvian gunpowder (with sodium nitrate) which was adopted as standard across the gunpowder-making industry in this country.[119]

Table 16 James Lobb, Powdermill Cottage, 1861

James Lobb	Head	48	Manager of powder works	Egloshayle, Cornwall,
Charity	Wife	45		Plymouth, Devon
Flora	Female	7	Scholar	Lydford, Devon
Rose	Female	5	Scholar	Lydford, Devon
Louisa	Female	3		Lydford, Devon

Having secured his position as manager (Table 16), James, like his older brother, was keen to improve the mixture of gunpowder. The *London Gazette* reported on 8 November 1861 that a patent had been awarded to:

> James Lobb, of the Gunpowder Works, Dartmoor, in the county of Devon, for the invention of 'improvements in gunpowder suitable for blasting'.[120]

Considering James had begun his career as a barrel-maker in Cornwall, he had evidently done well, as by 1861 he was in charge of a major works and was publicly recognised as having made improvements to the production of gunpowder.[121] However, the census of 1871 shows that James left the industry as he and his family are recorded as living in Plymouth where he is described as a 'ship owner'.[122]

Robert Williams and Charles Williams Jnr

When Charles Williams Snr bought the company in 1871 (Chapter 2) he instated his nephew Robert Williams and his own son Charles Williams Jnr as managers. Charles most probably worked from the company's Plymouth office while his cousin Robert moved himself and his family into the manager's accommodation to oversee the actual production of gunpowder.[123] It was during this period of joint management that the company was prosecuted for the first time for bad storage practices as the following report in *The Tavistock Gazette* reveals:

15 March 1872

Caution to Gunpowder Manufacturers – Charles Williams and Robert Williams, managers of the Dartmoor Gunpowder Manufactory, were summoned under the 23 and 24 Vic c. 139 'for that they did on the 6th of February last at Lydford have and keep in the corning and granulating house of the manufactory, for the purpose of being corned and granulated, 4,199 lbs of gunpowder, being 1,412 lbs in excess of the quantity allowed to be kept by law at any one time'. Second charge, 'with having on the same date kept in the press house, at Cherrybrook, in Lydford, 4,180 lbs of gunpowder, being 1,940 lbs in excess of the quantity allowed to be kept by law'. Third charge, 'for wilfully neglecting and delaying to move with due diligence a large quantity of finished gunpowder made by them weighting 25,000 lbs, which was then in the packaging room, from thence to the store'.

For obvious safety reasons there were legal restrictions on how much gunpowder could be kept in one place, which posed quite a challenge for the managers of gunpowder works. The factories had to keep producing to keep their workers employed and cost-effective, but if sales dropped this could cause an accumulation of stock. If the weather was bad, and the roads unusable, the company could not always get the gunpowder out to the intended customers and the gunpowder would stockpile in the factory. This may go some way to explaining why the inspectors

Colonel Vivian Dering Majendie, explosives expert ILLUSTRATION NETTY

Colonel Vivian Majendie (see Chapter 6) and Captain Smith in 1872 found such large amounts of gunpowder on site towards the end of winter.

The report goes on to criticise the conditions found in the factory:

Colonel Vivian Majendie, RA, one of Her Majesty's inspectors of gunpowder works, described the unsatisfactory state in which he found the works on the 6th February last, when he visited them with

Capt. Smith. Their objective was to protect life and if the defendants adopted the precautions required the Bench might not impose the full penalty... Mr Charles Williams consented to undertake that the rules as suggested should be carried out.[124]

Robert and Charles pleaded guilty and were given a reduced fine of £32 18s 8d.

Despite the prosecution, Robert and Charles Williams kept their jobs.[125] Robert's sons were also given work as carpenters at the factory, but shortly after the 1881 census they left the gunpowder mills to find work in Holbeton. In the same year Charles Snr, the owner of the factory, died. This and the declining fortunes of the company resulted in Robert leaving his post and sometime around 1882 he moved his family to Tavistock where he set up a business as a timber merchant and cooper, going on to become a manufacturer of mineral water and ginger beer.

A Williams waggon in Tavistock SOURCE RODERICK MARTIN

As a result Charles Jnr became both owner and manager of the gunpowder-making factory. Few company documents have survived, but an order for gunpowder in 1895 bears the signature of Charles Williams. There is also an order dated 1884 from Charles on behalf of the company to W.J. Woollcome for the purchase of trees. The company address on this document is Plympton St Mary, where Charles and his family are recorded as living in 1881 with their four sons and two servants. This suggests that the company could no longer afford an office in Plymouth and Charles was working from an address close to home. This is supported by an advert in the *Western Morning News* in 1882, which states that a delivery book belonging to a carter employed by the Plymouth and Dartmoor Gunpowder Company has been lost and that there would be a reward given if it was handed in to the Ridgway Saw Mills in Plympton.[126]

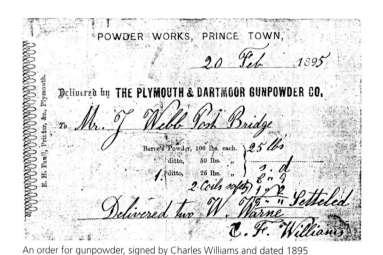

An order for gunpowder, signed by Charles Williams and dated 1895
TOM GREEVES COLLECTION

It seems that Charles also continued to be involved in other income-generating activities. For example, in 1881, he is listed in the census returns as a shipbuilder and a report in the theatre newspaper, *The Era*, in 1885, provides an account of him managing and leasing the Theatre Royal, where he was in charge of renovations costing more than £1000.[127] Did Charles get involved with the Plymouth theatre because he recognised there was no future in gunpowder production? Was he simply following his dream of managing a theatre? Did the factory's profitability suffer because its owner was too preoccupied with the theatre?

Sometime prior to 1891 Charles moved his family into the manager's accommodation at Powdermills, yet in the census of that year, despite still managing the factory, he is recorded as living with two servants in Torridge and described as a 'Timber merchant'. His wife Kezia and

was capable of making a strong argument. At a court case where George was called to give evidence concerning the East Cornwall Gunpowder Company's application for a licence to erect 'new mills, proper offices and magazines', he stated that by 1849 the Plymouth and Dartmoor Gunpowder Company had in full operation 'seven new magazines near towns'.[143] A newspaper advert in 1877 concerning the sale of a house and its surrounding land in Pembrokeshire called Carew Newton provides some information about how the gunpowder company paid for their magazines, as it stated that the property included a gunpowder magazine leased by the Plymouth and Dartmoor company on a sixty-year lease of which fifty remained at a rent of £4 a year.[144] Evidence has come to light of six magazines used by the company: Pocombe Bridge near Exeter, Efford in Plymouth, Wolborough Brake near Newton Abbot, Taviton near Tavistock, Summerhill near Ashburton and the aforementioned one in Carew, South Wales. The only known magazine that survives, albeit a ruin, is at Taviton.[145]

Gunpowder agents

The manufactured gunpowder was often sold through gunpowder agents/merchants such as Mr A. Francis of Tavistock.[146] The first recorded agent was William Lobb, who went on to become the factory manager. Agents were normally middlemen operating independently between manufacturers and customers. However, Lobb was clearly an employee as he lived in a company property. Gunpowder agents normally had other business activities as indicated by the very small number of people in the census returns for England and Wales that give their profession as gunpowder agents.[147] One agent was Thomas B. Tyeth, who was also a partner of the Plymouth and Dartmoor Gunpowder Company. In the newspaper report that lists the company's first proprietors, Thomas is described as an accountant, but it appears that his involvement with the gunpowder-making company also allowed him the opportunity to branch into selling powder as in 1861 he is listed as a 'Gunpowder Agent' in Plymouth. Yet, by 1871 (the same year the Williams family took over the company) he is described as a 'Retired Gunpowder Agent'.[148]

Little is known about how these middle men operated within the industry. Occasionally they would advertise in newspapers, as did Edward Pearce in 1872:

> *The Plymouth and Dartmoor Gunpowder Company… to inform MINE AGENTS and other Parties who may require BLASTING POWDER that they have always a Stock of the best quality in their Magazine in Par from which orders can be executed without delay.*
>
> *Agent for the company Mr Edward Pearce, Biscovery, Par Station.*[149]

There is also evidence of a case at the Court of Stannaries for Cornwall and Devon, where the Plymouth and Dartmoor Gunpowder Company accused Messrs Brunton and Co. (patent fuse manufacturers from Pool) of not paying a bill of £54 that had been owed for over two years. This report provides a wealth of information concerning how the company used agents, in this case Mr C. Webb of Chacewater. A brief outline of the facts concerning this complicated dispute is as follows:

• Two years prior to the court case Webb (the agent) gave Brunton and Co (a fuse company) Dartmoor gunpowder in exchange for fuses.[150]

• The Plymouth and Dartmoor Gunpowder Company were not informed of this exchange, therefore technically Webb had stolen the gunpowder to acquire these fuses which would be easier to sell (less bulky).

• As a result of his own financial mismanagement Webb later becomes bankrupt at which point the gunpowder company realised they hadn't been paid for the gunpowder supplied by Webb to Brunton and Co.

• Webb claims that he had sold the gunpowder to Brunton and Co. on behalf of the gunpowder company, and so they asked the fuse-making company to settle their bill, who refuse stating that their transaction was with Webb and he'd been paid in fuses.

• The gunpowder company reduce their bill to £50 to allow it be tried in the small claims court.

• After numerous examinations and cross examinations of various witnesses (notably the agent, the accused and the gunpowder company), the jury finds Brunton and Co. not guilty of non-payment of bill. It is not known what further action was taken by the company or the courts against Webb.

The report tells us much about the sales process within the gunpowder industry. It describes how the company used many agents all over the country and in this case they were 'in the habit of entrusting Webb with large quantities of gunpowder'.[151] Webb had represented the Dartmoor gunpowder producers for over twelve years and claimed that he never worked for any other gunpowder company or sold it in his own name. He describes how he was also 'in the habit of selling safety fuses on his own account' (which explains why he exchanged the gunpowder for them) and was employed as a purser for the following tin mines: South Tresavean, North Treskerby, North Jane and South Wheal Kitty.[152] For Webb's services to the gunpowder company he was paid 5 percent of the total sales. In 1860 he was charging £26 for 1000lbs and details of his sales had to be sent to the company every month.[153]

The report also states that Thomas B. Tyeth (one-time accountant, part owner of the gunpowder company and gunpowder agent himself), had become the company secretary of the Plymouth and Dartmoor Gunpowder Company and much of the evidence produced for the plaintiffs was supplied by his letters and personal testimonies.[154]

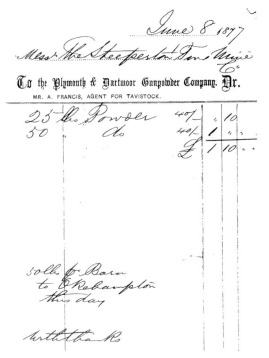

Documentation concerning the purchase of gunpowder
TOM GREEVES COLLECTION

CHAPTER 6
The factory site and the management of water

The general appearance of buildings is unsatisfactory in the extreme. They are dingy and comparatively uncared for, and the whole factory, to express myself plainly, has a 'starved' and careless appearance.[155]

Colonel Vivian Dering Majendie, RA, Chief Inspector of Explosives, describing the Powdermills factory in 1884

Dartmoor has always been an industrious place. Over the centuries its inhabitants have learnt how to produce a variety of goods such as tin, ice, arsenic, china clay, wool and paper from raw materials found on or under the ground.[156] The land upon which the factory was constructed had a history of industrial activity as 'in the valley bottom can be found extensive remains of earlier tin streaming activity'.[157] The raw materials needed to produce gunpowder, on the other hand, had to be brought in. As gunpowder had never been made on the moor before, the company had to turn to 'outsiders' to design the works and provide the necessary expertise regarding its production. What Dartmoor did have, however, was an abundance of water to provide the factory with power. It also had a long history of efficient water management.

The factory in operation

In total the Powdermills site covered 33 hectares with the factory buildings concentrated within about 9 hectares. Research suggests that 'the design of the Powdermills plant and the "know-how" of gunpowder manufacture was probably provided by the Fox and Perran Foundry in Perranwharf' in Cornwall.[158] When in operation, it involved mills, waterwheels, roads, bridges, storerooms, service buildings, homes for the workers and a system of leats and reservoirs.[159] Much, if not all of the granite used for these structures was extracted in the immediate locality, as four quarries have been located within the site.[160] Granite was ideal for a gunpowder factory as the buildings had to be strong enough to withstand the potential force of an explosion. The roofs were made out of timber and tarpaulin so that the blast could be directed up rather than out, and remnants of tar used to make the roofs waterproof can still be found on some of the masonry.[161] Unfortunately nothing is known about who built the factory or the numbers involved, but it seems likely that Postbridge and Princetown would have supplied a large proportion of the workforce.

The task of making gunpowder required three basic ingredients: sulphur from Sicily, saltpetre (sodium nitrate) from South America and charcoal.[162] Coal and/or peat also had to be brought in as it was needed to heat the boilers. Making gunpowder involved numerous processes, and a report carried out by English Heritage provides a good overall description of the workings of the site on Dartmoor:

> Amongst the buildings identified at Powder Mills are: grinding mills, where the ingredients were crushed separately between horizontal rotating millstones; blending mills, where the ingredients were mixed in rotating barrels; incorporation mills, where the material from the blending mills was mixed further into a single compound; a range of buildings where the gunpowder was broken, pressed, corned, dried, dusted and glazed; and finally charge magazines, where the gunpowder was stored. Further buildings on the site may have been used as storage or office accommodation.[163]

Working at the factory was tough – there was no modern-day conveyor belt moving things through the site.[164] At each stage of production the powder labourers had to collect and then move the mixture (presumably in sacks) from one building to another in wooden hand carts. Once the gunpowder was finally made it had to be placed into barrels of various sizes and taken off-site to be stored in the company magazine which was situated away from the main site and most of the workers' houses. However, buildings sometimes referred to in the censuses as 'Powder Mill Cottages West' were constructed near the gunpowder store, and it may have been that the inhabitants of these homes were responsible for safeguarding the barrels against theft.

What was it like to work in this environment? Think of the dust and dirt, the isolation, the weather, the mist, the smells, the sight of the many waterwheels turning and the sound of creaking gears, and behind the chat and banter a degree of fear and an awareness that gunpowder was volatile and dangerous and one small mistake could cost lives. The workers had to get through each day knowing that at any moment they could be injured or killed, often suffering a slow and painful death. Perhaps the younger or less experienced employees did not give it much thought or were just blissfully ignorant, but the workers who had witnessed the injuries and deaths in 1851 and 1857 (Chapter 2), or had read newspapers report of fatalities in other gunpowder factories, would have been well aware of the dangers of working with gunpowder. However, dangerous and arduous work was par for the course for many working-class labourers in the nineteenth century.

Remains of cottages near the company's magazine

The factory inspections

Some of the best contemporary descriptions of the factory in operation are provided by inspections carried out in 1872 (see Chapter 5) and 1884 by Colonel Majendie RA, Chief Inspector of Explosives.[165] Majendie had lived an interesting life. He had joined the Royal Artillery in 1851, served with distinction at Sevastopol during the Crimean War, liberated the besieged Lucknow during the Indian Mutiny, wrote articles on explosives for the press and worked for the police as a bomb disposal expert. He was also related to the 'Jack the Ripper' suspect Montague Druitt, whose name became linked to the atrocities following his death in 1888, the year the killings ceased. A strong case has been made for Druitt being responsible for the murders. The man leading the investigation at Scotland Yard was Sir Melville Macnaghton who was a good friend of Majandie and it has been suggested that Macnaghton deliberately withheld information concerning Druitt's involvement to protect the reputation of Majendie and his family.[166]

The Colonel was employed by the government to inspect all gunpowder factories and his reports of the works on Dartmoor were critical. In 1884 the *Tavistock Gazette* reported on a court case where the owner Charles Williams Jnr was accused of not keeping the factory in a proper working order.[167] During the proceedings, the contents of a letter from the Colonel to Charles Williams Jnr was read which contained numerous criticisms:

A glazing house at the factory not properly lined and constructed... Many acts of gross negligence... The condition of the factory was generally unsatisfactory for the manufacture of gunpowder...

It then goes into more detail:

Packing House – The floor boards are open at the joints in several instances, particularly near one of the doors, and between these joints earth and dirt and accumulated powder are visible and can be easily extracted; one open joint was three quarters of an inch wide and actually in one place blades of grass were sprouting between the boards. The wood lining was very defective. This in some places does not come down to the floor, and grit from behind is easily shaken down; and at one of the windows it is shrunk away from the wall, and there is a wide, open space below the window sill, which space is full of dirt... The building is very far from being as well swept as it should be, and the neglect in this respect is evidenced by cobwebs behind the doors, in corners, and on the ceiling. Part of the hooks of the scale and beam of uncovered iron are also exposed... The saltpetre bin projects into an unlined room, and is quite unsuitable and insufficient for the protection of the men... Stove – The interior or stove proper has, I observed a bare slate floor, from which (mingled with the powder) it was easy to pick up detached particles of slate and grit. There was a hole in the floor of the ante-chamber...

Express Magazine – The floor of this building is very imperfect and ill-laid, and many openings in it.

And so the list goes on. Summing up his letter the inspector states that in relation to a previous inspection:

I consider that it has distinctly gone backwards rather than advanced, and I am not prepared to take the responsibility of allowing such a state of things and a long list of defects such as I have enumerated above to continue. It is my intention to lay the matter before the Secretary of State with a view to proceedings being instituted against you for such of the offences as may be advised.

Charles Williams Jnr responded to Colonel Majendie's accusations:

We regret to find you should have thought it necessary to find such a long list of faults. To have mentioned them to our manager, stating your wishes in regard to the matter, would have been sufficient to have induced us to having done our best to meet your views so far as to be considered reasonable. If all the allegations in your letter can be verified of course we should not hesitate to discharge at once the manager of the factory, and several employees in charge of the various buildings of which you complain, but have gone carefully into the matter and heard the explanations of the parties implicated, we consider that for the present this would be a most unfair step to take, having as we believe, a perfect and complete answer, both on their part and our own, to the almost innumerable charges which you bring against us, the effect of which is really only to harass the trade and drive it from the country… We take great exception to the tone of your letter as being personally offensive, and written in such a way as you cannot justify. Before concluding we think it right to state that we are now, as we have ever been, quite prepared to carry out any reasonable improvement, or make good and defects which may from time to time become necessary, when they are put before us in reasonable and temperate language; or the writer will personally meet you at any time you may appoint and go with you to the works, so that your wishes may be fully explained and our representative have an opportunity of laying his views before you.

The gunpowder company's solicitor Mr Edmonds then put forward a strong defence by criticising Colonel Majendie for not meeting Charles Williams face-to-face and questioned the inspector's expertise concerning gunpowder factories, following which a factory employee, Mr Bickle, was brought in on behalf of the defence to give evidence concerning the cleanliness of the factory.

In total the court proceedings lasted over five hours. Charles Williams was found guilty of seven of the fifteen charges and the magistrate gave the following sentence:

In each of the seven cases proved the defendant would be fined £2 and the costs, and the penalty would have been greater if many of the cases had not been so much alike, having been brought under section 10, rule 2. The fines amounted in the aggregate to £14, and the costs were £6 6s. If all the charges had been gone into and proved Mr Williams would have been liable to penalties amounting to £150, exclusive of costs.

The report of the exchanges between the inspector and the owner of the company do neither party any favours. Majendie comes across as being over-officious, while the management of the company appear slapdash. In defence of the inspector, the Colonel had many years' experience. He had been appointed 'Her Majesty's Inspector of Gunpowder Works' in 1870, and in a period of four years oversaw the inspection of 409 sites that were involved in the production or storage of gunpowder (only twenty-six were actual factories, most were magazines). His findings resulted in the 1875 Gunpowder Act and led to the Explosions Inspectorate being formed. The organisation did much to save lives:

> A crude index of its effectiveness may be obtained by comparing the years 1868–70, when an average of 43 people per year were killed, with the period 1885–1905, when the death rate reached double figures only three out of those 20 years. This despite threefold increase in the size of the industry.[168]

It is also important to note that the Plymouth and Dartmoor Gunpowder Company were found guilty of not keeping their factory in a proper order, thus putting their workers lives at risk. Whether the recommended changes were made following the court case is not known, but in the same year the *Dorset County Chronicle* reported:

> Some powder mills near Princetown Dartmoor were nearly destroyed by an explosion on Wednesday afternoon; but the workmen being absent, no one was killed.[169]

FINAL THOUGHTS

Who'd have thought these ruins were connected to cheesy biscuits, Prince Albert and monkey puzzle trees.

Drew Campbell, in conversation with his bored children, 2017

Making gunpowder on Dartmoor was a complicated and dangerous process, yet despite hardship, occasional court cases and accidents it was considered to be worth the effort and risk for those involved. George Frean worked tirelessly to promote and manage the Plymouth and Dartmoor Gunpowder Company during its early years, but the production of gunpowder on the moor was very much a collective effort involving investors, office staff, managers, agents, factory workers, carters and labourers. Furthermore, this was a venture that could not rely on local resources, knowledge and manpower. Some of the required money came from Cornwall and London, its raw materials came mostly from overseas and while some local labour was used, much of the workforce came from Cornwall and other counties.

Lewis Everly (1886–1971) pictured at Vitifer Mine around 1910. The boxes at his feet contained dynamite, the popularity of which contributed to the closure of the gunpowder factory. TOM GREEVES COLLECTION

The demand for gunpowder fell due to competition from dynamite (which appeared *c*.1867) and a slump in local demand. In 1897 the decision was taken to close the factory. It had been in operation for over fifty years, during which time the country – and the world – had undergone many changes. During the second half of the nineteenth century the 'old order' came under threat from those seeking reform in Britain. Women were becoming more involved with institutions such as Poor Law Boards, schools and local government, and Parliamentary reforms meant that by 1884 two thirds of men had the vote. Factory Acts from 1833 were introduced to improve working conditions and by the end of Queen Victoria's reign the

British Empire had expanded to a fifth of the earth's surface, yet the majority of the population of this country still lived in abject poverty.

In 1901, the year Queen Victoria died, four people are recorded living at the Powdermills properties despite the factory having been closed for four years. These included two members of the Bellamy family: George and his son William. Both men had lived at Powdermills since the 1850s, and as employees of the company they had witnessed the highs and lows of its fortunes. William Bellamy, who had been born at Powdermills, went on to marry the manager's daughter (see Chapter 4), but after the factory closed he and his father George (who was probably the company's longest-serving employee) became stockmen for a nearby farm. Both men raised families at the Powdermills but were widowed at a relatively young age. Yet, instead of remarrying and/or moving they chose to live together at their family home, even though the factory was no longer in operation.

Despite the company folding on Charles Williams Jnr's 'watch', he continued leasing the land and property up until his death.[171] In April 1903 Williams (writing from the Grand Theatre in Plymouth where he is described as both lessee and manager), wrote to the Duchy's steward asking for a reduction in his rent at 'Dartmoor Powder Works Estate', arguing that 'I don't think it is worth so much as I have been paying'. He further explains:

My late Father took the lease when the property was worked as a Gunpowder Factory, but as this industry has been practically killed by the introduction of other explosives and the unnecessary interference of Government inspectors, the property is now only of agricultural and residential value.[172]

In August of the same year Williams wrote again to the Duchy concerning the length of his lease, and describes his plans for the derelict gunpowder works:

I have been giving the matter further consideration as to how the property might best be utilised and an idea has occurred to me of making it a health resort or Sanatorium and I think I should be disposed to try it, but it will take a considerable outlay, and that there would be no possibility of recouping with such a short term.[173]

Unfortunately for Williams his dream never materialised and four years later he writes again to the Duchy informing them about his plans for Sunnyside Cottages and some other buildings to be 'allowed to go down'. Presumably they were not being used and beyond repair. He also reveals that much of the workings were still on site:

> *What I should suggest is that I should dispose of the old machinery (which is now useless) in the Powder Factory and that the material of some buildings should be utilised in filling up the hole and excavations which were made for the waterwheels etc., so as to make it safe and that some of the Buildings (which might possibly be useful) should be maintained at any rate, so far as the walls and roofs are concerned and also that the dwelling house occupied by Mr Saltoun and the Cottages near should be repaired and new lease granted to me at £40 for 7 or 14 years.*[174]

The Duchy agreed to his terms and Williams continued to make a profit from the estate through renting out properties and fields.

In September 1917 the Duchy Office received a letter informing them that C.F. Williams had passed away and that a certain Miss Pearse was his 'sole Executrix'.[175] In the census of 1911, six years prior to Williams' death, the residents of Church Cottage, Yealmpton are listed as C.F. Williams (aged 64 and married) and a servant (Ellen Chaffe). There is also a 'visitor' recorded at the address: Miss L.M. Pearse (aged 50, living by private means). Clearly this was a long-term arrangement resulting in Miss Pearse, and not Williams' children, inheriting his estate. Miss Pearse continued with the Powdermills Estate with tenants such as Mrs Smith who is recorded as renting two cottages in 1917. In 1923 Miss Pearse surrendered her lease of Powdermills and tenants from this date appear to have dealt with the Duchy Office direct. These included Dr Atkins (1923), Ralph Michell (1929) and the Stephens family (1932).[176]

During the Second World War Powdermills was occupied by American troops. One source claims that around three thousand personnel were stationed there prior to the D-Day landings and some of them attempted to steal the factory's proving mortar (testing cannon), but were stopped at Plymouth.[177] This weapon was used to test the strength of the gunpowder

The Breaking House (12), and the remains of a stone table used for breaking up compressed gunpowder

APPENDIX 1
A tour of the site

Spending time exploring the Powdermills site is immensely rewarding, and the recommended route offered here will help you to make sense of the buildings and layout. Please note that there is no public right of way from the existing buildings to the gate at the bottom of the site where the tour starts. The fenced-off structures to the west of the Cherry Brook are on private land, and there is no public access to them.

The Lych Way (public bridlepath) crosses the B3212 northeast of Higher Cherrybrook Bridge. The path is signed to Powdermills at a gate and enters the top of the site not far from one of the Incorporation Mills (7). Follow the track downhill to cross the Cherry Brook, then turn left to reach the gate at the bottom of the site. The tour starts from this point.

Once in the site it is possible to reach the pottery gallery by passing through the small gate on the Lych Way near Chimney 1 (15). Turn left (across rough and often wet ground) and head south towards the existing buildings, eventually reaching a five-bar gate by the gallery. Alternatively visitors to the pottery gallery can ask for directions to the Lych Way and Chimney 1.

Research papers by the archaeologist Andrew Pye in 1994 and the scientist Bob Ashford in 2014 and 2017 have made great strides in furthering our understanding of how the site 'worked'.[183] Using their findings as a foundation, let's take a look at the Powdermills' structures and their function, and where possible consider each building in the order in which the raw materials moved through the factory.[184] The map shown here will help navigation around the site.

The best place to begin this 'tour' is from the gate at the southern end of the site (see map).[185] This is where all the raw materials came in and the newly made gunpowder went out.[186] Ahead is a track, with numerous structures on the left.[187]

Before heading up the track there is another site to see, located a little further away from the west bank of the Cherry Brook. This is on

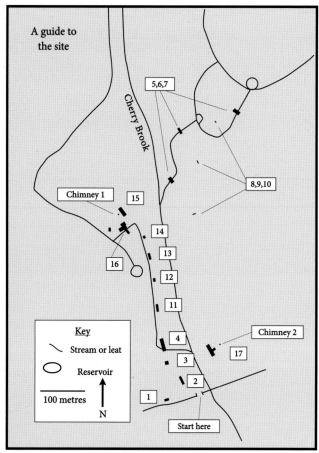

A simplified map of Powdermills factory site

The factory track

private land, but the remains of the building can be seen over the first gate on the left.

1 CHECKING HOUSE

Here workers were inspected before entering the site – mainly to ensure they had nothing on them that could ignite the gunpowder – anything from sparking hobnailed boots to tobacco (see Chapter 1). If there was a signing-in system, it would mostly likely have taken place here. It may also have

Checking House (foreground)

been used as a changing room.

Head up the track, passing a line of buildings on the left, all on private land.

2 WATCH HOUSE

From this building the movement of raw materials (coming in) and finished gunpowder (going out) could be monitored, and it is possible that materials were also stored here. This is where the site was supervised. Hand barrows, used to transport the gunpowder around the site, were

Watch House

probably stored in the left side of the structure. This area may also have been used as a waiting room/safe space for workers.

3 STORE ROOM

The lack of fireplaces, windows or a wheelpit suggests this building was used for storage.

Possible store room

4 PREPARATION ROOMS

Here the ingredients for making gunpowder were milled (notice the two wheelpits). The room on the left is where charcoal and sulphur were ground down. The middle part of the building was used for storage, sieving and weighing the powder. It was then moved to the room on the right, where it was put into barrels and churned into what was referred to as the 'green charge'. This is the stage at which the production process started to become dangerous.

Preparation rooms

The site was probably designed so that all the processing of the gunpowder took place on the west bank of the Cherry Brook. However, as Chapter 2 reveals there wasn't enough water in the Cherry Brook to power all the waterwheels on the west bank so an additional leat from the East Dart river had to be constructed to supply the factory with more water. As this extra water power came in on the east bank, this meant that the Incorporation Mills (5,6,7) had to be sited there.[189] While this change in plan fixed the problem, it disrupted the line of production. Instead of everything simply being moved from building to building along the west bank of the stream, halfway through the process the green charge had to be moved by labourers across the bridge up the hill to these mills.

Follow the track to the right, across the Cherry Brook, and head uphill towards the Incorporation Mills (5,6,7), and imagine workers having to negotiate the steady incline with a heavy load. Clearly this was a necessity, but it would have slowed production and increased both the workload and risk to the workers.

5,6,7 INCORPORATION MILLS

Here water was added to the green charge, and further milling took place. This was one of the most dangerous stages of the process, especially during the stopping and starting of the machinery. Overshot waterwheels provided the power to grind down the ingredients. The mill walls were plastered to make cleaning easier. Remnants of plaster can be seen, along with drips of tar which was used to waterproof the canvas roof.[190]

Above the top Incorporation Mill (7) can be found the remains of a reservoir, constructed at the highest point in the site.

The Cherry Brook PHOTOGRAPH ADRIAN TAYLOR

The foundations of three other buildings can also be found in this area:

8,9,10 EXPENSE MAGAZINES

These were stores for gunpowder before (green charge) and after (ripe charge) it was worked in the Incorporation Mills.

Having been worked in the Incorporation Mills (and possibly stored in the Expense Magazines) the ripe charge was then brought back down the hill and across the bridge to be further processed in the buildings on the west side of the site.

11 PRESS HOUSE

Next the gunpowder was put into a press, which was driven by a waterwheel, to squeeze out any moisture.

12 BREAKING HOUSE

Here slabs of compressed gunpowder were broken up into various sizes on a stone 'table' (part of which still exists).

Incorporation Mill (7)

Press House

Breaking House

13 CORNING HOUSE

Here the 'pieces' of gunpowder were sieved and separated into different sizes. The fine gunpowder was returned to the Press House and the oversized pieces were returned to the Breaking House.

14 STORE

This is probably were the corns (sieved gunpowder) was stored.

15 CHIMNEY 1 AND SURROUNDING BUILDINGS

In the building to the east of the chimney the gunpowder was heated and dried out prior to packing. A boiler was in operation and excess smoke dispersed by the chimney.

16 FINAL PREPARATION ROOMS

Experts agree that this area is difficult to understand. It is believed that here the gunpowder was dusted, glazed, sieved and packed, then loaded onto carts to be moved off-site. It may also have

Corning House

Store

Chimney 1

been where barrels, fuel, wood, materials and various other provisions were stored, and horses/ ponies were stabled.

The finished gunpowder was taken back along the

Final preparation rooms (near Chimney 1)

track and through the gates to the company magazine closer to the main road, where it would await collection by carters for delivery to customers or company magazines.

Another substantial structure stands on the east bank of the Cherry Brook:

17 CHIMNEY 2 AND SURROUNDING BUILDINGS

Opinion differs as to what went on here: it has been suggested that if charcoal was made on site this is probably where it took place. It has also been suggested that ready-made charcoal was brought in and that these structures were 'used for processing and storing saltpetre'.

Chimney 2 and some of the surrounding buildings

It is unfortunate that there is no surviving map labelling what each structure did, as there are for some gunpowder works. Trying to understand the site is further complicated by buildings changing their function (which explains why so many doors and windows are blocked up). Much of the site remains a mystery and there has to be an element of educated guesswork in the interpretation of how the factory operated. Hopefully this guide will help you to get a feel for how the process worked, but for a more detailed account of the site please consult the previously mentioned studies of Andrew Pye and Bob Ashford.

APPENDIX 2
The use of water

In this country today, we are fortunate to have clean water piped directly into our homes. We also have electricity at a flick of a switch. We have to some extent forgotten how important water has been, not only to sustain us, but also as a power source. Throughout the country there are numerous abandoned gunpowder works, where among the ruins can be seen the remnants of this technology: pits for waterwheels, derelict machinery, leats and grinding stones. Clearly the industry up until the twentieth century was dependent on water power, and Dartmoor was no exception.

There is a long history of managing water to power machinery on Dartmoor. The earliest evidence can be found in the Domesday Book where a number of mills are listed.[193] During medieval times corn mills became a common sight on the moor and over

One of many wheelpits on the site PHOTOGRAPH KEITH RYAN

time people found other ways of managing water to make goods such as cloth, leather, paper, tin and edge tools. These wonderful examples of hydro-engineering provided the necessary water to power these mills, and supplied communities on and off the moor with water for domestic use.

The management of water often brings people together as it can be labour-intensive and often requires the likes of landowners and water users such as farmers and millers to cooperate. Water management can also be a cause for conflict, as exemplified by the many instances of disputes caused by Dartmoor tinners silting up existing watercourses and diverting their flow. However, no evidence has so far been found of disagreements caused by the gunpowder works' extensive water governance.

A waterwheel still in use on Dartmoor at the National Trust's Finch Foundry in Sticklepath
PHOTOGRAPH RICHARD PAUL WILSON WATCHTHEBIRDIEWILDLIFEPHOTOGRAPHY.COM

Such was the complexity of water use at the Dartmoor gunpowder factory that there is insufficient space in this book to do the subject justice. Instead I have provided a simplified version of the process.

The factory's buildings and waterwheels (in wheelpits) were constructed in a line alongside the Cherry Brook. Some of the water from this watercourse was diverted to a reservoir so that the flow to the waterwheels could be controlled.[194] Any excess was channelled either to the next wheel or back into the watercourse. As there was insufficient water in the Cherry Brook to drive the numerous wheels an additional source was brought in from the East Dart river. The map of the works (see Appendix 1) reveals how three leats supplied the various mills with water (two from the Cherry Brook and one from the East Dart river). These leats fed two/three reservoirs which supplied the water (via other leats that were controlled with sluice gates) to at least seven waterwheels, with the excess water running back into the Cherry Brook.[195]

The production of gunpowder on Dartmoor required an extensive system of water governance, but it was not without its challenges. Supplies had to be maintained during dry periods and it was important that the Cherry Brook was not allowed to flood in times of heavy rain. Despite being abandoned for over a hundred years, the leat from the East Dart river can still be followed and in some places remains in remarkable condition with some evidence of the working mechanisms that controlled the water flow. It is also possible to follow the line of other leats which were part of the factory's water system.

Sluice-gate mechanism found in the leat near Archerton House
PHOTOGRAPH DREW CAMPBELL

The builders of the gunpowder factory also constructed bridges to allow people to cross the Cherry Brook, and culverts (water tunnels) to allow watercourses to pass under access tracks. Good examples of these structures can be seen along the track towards the abandoned magazine.

Culvert under the access track leading to the company magazine

The following is an excellent description by Eric Hemery of how water was used at the factory, and highlights how steps were taken to clean the water before it was given back to nature:

> The leating system was ingenious, and the water-wheel houses were massively built, the leats first having fed a reservoir situated near the highest (eastern) wheel-house. After passing through the wheel-pits, the water was somewhat polluted and was 'tail-raced' for some way down the valley as a cleansing measure before being allowed to join the Cherry Brook. This entailed its twice crossing *under* the brook, first by wooden conduit and then by a large one of granite downstream. Modern industrial undertakings show less environmental concerns. [196]

It is worth also noting that water was needed by the residents of Powdermills for domestic use. An undated map of the site found in the Duchy Office shows a spring close to the building which is now the Pottery Gallery, and a pipeline to the track that leads to the magazine.

REFERENCES

1 G. Fabian Miller, *Home: Dartmoor* (Newton Abbot, 2012), p. 124. During conversations with Gary Fabian Miller, Tom Greeves, the cultural environmentalist, provides this description of Dartmoor: 'The landscape itself is probably one of the richest cultural landscapes in the whole world, in terms of the millennia of human presence that you can observe tangibly within it'.

2 J. Hassan, *A History of Water in Modern England and Wales* (Manchester, 1993): 'Water has, until recently been a fairly neglected area of historical investigation', p. 1. See also V.L. Scarborough, 'Water management adaptations in non-industrial complex societies: an archaeological perspective', *Archaeological Method and Theory*, 3 (1991), pp. 108-115, regarding the 'four principle techniques' of water manipulation: wells, reservoirs, dams and canals.

3 A. Marwick, *The New Nature of History: Knowledge, Evidence, Language* (Basingstoke, 2001), p. 32.

4 F. Pryor, *The Making of the British Landscape: How We Have Transformed the Land from Prehistory to Today* (London, 2010), p. 20.

5 For an account of Natural England's policy on overgrazing see T. Greeves, 'Dartmoor and the Displacement of Culture: Analysis and Remedy', *Transactions of the Devonshire Association for the Advancement of Science, Literature and the Arts*, 147 (2015), pp. 15-7 and p. 37.

6 H. Harris, *The Industrial Archaeology of Dartmoor* (1968, Newton Abbot, 1992), pp. 128-133, A.R. Pye, 'An Example of a Non-metalliferous Dartmoor Industry: the Gunpowder Factory at Powdermills', in D.M. Griffiths (ed.) *The Archaeology of Dartmoor: Perspectives from the 1990's* (Stroud, 1996), A.R. Pye, and R. Robinson, *An Archaeological Survey of the Gunpowder Factory at Powdermills Farm, Postbridge, Dartmoor* (Exeter, 1990), F. Booker, 'Industry' in C. Gill (ed.), *Dartmoor: A New Study* (Newton Abbot, 1977), P. Newman, *The Field Archaeology of Dartmoor* (Swindon, 2011), A. Brunton, *The Gunpowder Mills: Dartmoor* (1994, Newton Abbot, 1999), E. Hemery, *High Dartmoor: Land and People* (1983, London, 1992), pp. 435-7, B. Ashford, 'Some thoughts on Dartmoor Powder Mills', *Transactions of the Devonshire Association for the Advancement of Science, Literature and the Arts*, 146 (2014).

7 A. Leftwich, 'Politics: people, resources and power', in A. Leftwich (ed.), *What is Politics? The Activity and Study* (1984, Oxford, 1988), p. 63.

8 The report was originally printed in *Godey's Lady's Book,* 1861. It was given to P.

Merrick and subsequently published in *Gunpowder Mills Study Group Newsletter* 21 (August, 1997), p. 14. The silhouette of the worker and all other silhouettes are provided with kind permission by Rita of Clipartqueen, see http://www.clipartqueen.com/about-clipartqueen.html.

[9] G. Best, *Mid-Victorian Britain, 1851-75* (1971, St Albans, 1987), p. 99: During the mid-eighteenth century a third of the population were involved in manufacturing.

[10] See T. Greeves, *Called Home – The Dartmoor Tin Miner, 1860-1940* (Truro, 2016), p. 66, for a description of tin miners breakfast being tea, bread and cream. Occasionally he would have 'kittle broth' which was bread covered in hot water with added butter: Miners would also sometimes start the day with cake.

[11] Harris, *Industrial Archaeology of Dartmoor*, p. 132. In the 1891 Census, Silas Sleep (25) is recorded as being from Cornwall, living at Lodge Cottage with his wife Harriet (27) and his five month old daughter Harriet. In 1901, four years after Powdermills closed he is listed as a tin miner with his wife and four children (including twins). Evidently he survived working at the factory. See D. J. Oddy, 'Food, Drink and Nutrition' in F.M.L. Thompson (ed.), *The Cambridge Social History of Britain: 1750-1950, Volume II: People and their Environment* (Cambridge, 1990): 'Eating three meals a day was the accepted pattern everywhere in Britain by the eighteenth century', p. 257.

[12] There is some debate over where Sunnyside Cottages were.

[13] Hemery, *High Dartmoor*, p. 437.

[14] Following the 1875 Explosions Act all employees of gunpowder works had to be searched every morning. See English Heritage, *An Archaeological Survey, Research Department Report Services no 63 – 2009, Gatebeck Low Gunpowder Works and the workers settlement of Endmoor and Gatebeck, Cumbria*, p. 102.

[15] See Anon, 'Schultze Gunpowder Factory.' http://www.thenewforestguide.co.uk/history/new-forest-explosives/schultze-gunpowder-factory/ (07/10/2016), for an account of workers in the Schultze factory in the New Forest being searched every morning.

[16] G. Crocker, *The Gunpowder Industry* (Haverfordwest, 2002), p. 22: 'The worst were multiple accidents such as that at Kames in Argyll in 1863 in which a granulating house, press house, glazing house, dusting house, double press house and glazing house exploded in succession killing seven men and injuring eight others'.

[17] Anon, 'Glyn-Neath Gunpowder Works, Pontneddfechan.' http://www.breconbeacons.org/glyn-neath-gunpowder-works-pontneddfechan

(1/9/2016): 'Safety was paramount and all possible precautions to avoid explosions were taken. Employees had to change into work clothes before entering potentially dangerous areas'.

[18] Greeves, *Called Home – The Dartmoor Tin Miner*, p. 34.

[19] *Macclesfield Courier*, 4/6/1836.

[20] *High Peek News*, 26/10/1892. The reporters took the account of this event (which had occurred 4 May 1848) from a pamphlet which had been written by the victim's work-mate J. Taylor, who was selling it at 1d and giving the money to the widow.

[21] *Bell's Weekly Messenger*, 19/7/1851, p. 5.

[22] *North Devon Journal*, 12/2/1857, p. 3. In the same month, two men (possibly employees of the company at their magazine on the outskirts of the city) were injured by gunpowder: 'James Endicott 51 and James Endicott Jun., 19 – burns received from the explosion of gunpowder, which ignited by a spark from a candle as they shifted it from one bay to another,' see *Exeter and Plymouth Gazette*, 21/2/1857, p. 5.

[23] *Western Times*, 21/11/1857, p. 6.

[24] *Western Times*, 26/12/1857, p. 6.

[25] Of the two named workers who died in the December blast, Dodd does not register on the 1851 census at or near Powdermills, whereas there are two Hamlyns listed off-site – both living at separate addresses: Thomas aged 29 and Elias aged 25.

[26] See Censuses for 1851 and 1861.

[27] From Anon, 'Murrays World.' http://www.murraysworld.com/forum/chit-chat/spooks-spectres-and-the-supernatural/135/ (2/1/2017). As entertaining as this story is, it has to be noted that there is significant doubt about its authenticity and to date no evidence has emerged that the factory ever employed an Italian.

[28] Best, *Mid-Victorian Britain*, p. 137.

[29] *Gunpowder Mills Study Group Newsletter* 21 (August, 1997), p. 16: The description was taken from a contemporary report of a visit to an unnamed gunpowder factory in 1861.

[30] *High Peak News*, 4/7/1874. The ruins now lie beneath Fernilee Reservoir.

[31] English Heritage, 'Gatebeck Low Gunpowder Works and the workers settlement of Endmoor and Gatebeck, Cumbria', in *An Archaeological Survey, Research Department Report Services* 63 (2009), p. 105.

[32] Best, *Mid-Victorian Britain*, p. 41.

[33] Oddy, 'Food, Drink and Nutrition', pp. 255-61. Following the 'hungry forties' Oddy states 'food prices began to fall from the end of the second decade of the

nineteenth century', p. 253. W. Crossing, *Crossing's A Hundred Years on Dartmoor* (1901, Newton Abbot, 1971), p. 91: Crossing describes the usual food of Dartmoor peasant as being 'nothing better than barley bread, potatoes, with broth and bacon, and such vegetables as leeks and onions'.

[34] Oddy, 'Food, Drink and Nutrition', p. 265.

[35] Crossing, *A Hundred Years on Dartmoor,* p. 95-6.

[36] Sometime around 1889 the pub became 'Webb's Temperance Hotel', therefore anyone wanting an alcoholic drink would have had to have continued up to the Warren House Inn. I am grateful to Tom Greeves for pointing out that there was another drinking establishment at Postbridge at Smallwaters, known as 'The Good Intent', but it is not known when it was operating. See T. Sandles, 'Ghostly Bloodhound.' http://www.legendarydartmoor.co.uk/ghostly-bloodhound.htm (7/10/2016).

[37] While some workers were happy to partake in the public houses' medicinal qualities, it is fair to assume that the factory management were keen to dissuade excessive drinking for obvious safety reasons.

[38] Brunton, *Gunpowder Mills: Dartmoor*, p. 16. Hemery, *High Dartmoor,* pp. 435-6: The public house in question was the Greyhound Inn in Postbridge, which is no longer standing. Greyhound Farm was later built on the site of the inn.

[39] Crossing, *A Hundred Years on Dartmoor*, pp. 91-2.

[40] Crossing, *A Hundred Years on Dartmoor,* p. 92.

[41] *Royal Cornwall Gazette,* 13/7/1849, pp. 6-7.

[42] See Anon, 'Schultze Gunpowder Factory.' http://www.thenewforestguide.co.uk/history/new-forest-explosives/schultze-gunpowder-factory/ (07/10/2016).

[43] The National Archives, RG 4/428 (Cornwall: Launceston, Castle Street Chapel Births and Baptisms), 1793. Numerous sources state that he was born in 1794, but clearly this evidence shows it was 1793.

[44] In the same year George is listed as one of 32 constables in Plymouth, see Plymouth and West Devon Record Office, 1/352 (Devon, Plymouth Borough Records 1519-1905), 1816. See also House of Commons Papers, Reports from Committees: Corn Trade, Session 19 February-10 September, 1835, Vol 13, p. 19: Frean states under cross examination that he is a 'corn-factor and miller', and that he has held the office of 'Collector' at the Plymouth custom house department for ten years', p. 19. See also Crossing, *A Hundred Years on Dartmoor*, p. 57: Crossing states that Frean was an alderman and describes him as 'a man of great enterprise'.

[45] The numerous references to 'George Frean of Plymouth' in newspaper reports of his business activities indicate that the Freans were based in Plymouth for example see the *Western Times*, 21/10/1848, p. 3.

[46] See the *Western Times*, 3/5/1845, p. 1, where Frean is given permission by the Duke of Cornwall to cut peat on Dartmoor. For bone manure production see the *London Gazette*, 30/3/1860, p. 1277. For railways see the *Western Courier*, 1/12/1852, p. 4, where he is listed as a director in South Devon and Tavistock Railway Company.

[47] Not all of Frean's ventures where successful, but many were.

[48] P. Newman, *The Field Archaeology of Dartmoor* (Swindon, 2011), p. 181.

[49] J. Somers Cocks, 'Exploitation', in C. Gill (ed.) *Dartmoor: A New Study* (Newton Abbot, 1987), pp. 251-5. This account reveals how even though Tyrwhitt may have had honourable intentions, ultimately his attempts have to be considered failures. See also Newman, *The Field Archaeology of Dartmoor*, p. 181, where Newman describes how Tyrwhitt was 'a central character' in the movement towards improving Dartmoor's agriculture. In addition to his agricultural interests Thomas Tyrwhitt established on Dartmoor the settlement of Princetown and its prison and promoted the improvement of roads and the construction of railways.

[50] Somers Cocks, *Dartmoor*, p. 258.

[51] Hemery, *High Dartmoor*, p. 435: Frean appears to have got in trouble for not applying for a licence to cut a leat to the Mills and 'in February 1848 the matter was taken up by the Duchy Secretary; the suggested discussion necessitated another journey to London for Frean'.

[52] For Exeter see *Woolmer's Exeter and Plymouth Gazette*, 14/10/1848, p. 8. For Ashburton see the *Western Times*, 18/3/1848, p. 3.

[53] See A. Briggs, *The Age of Improvement, 1783-1867* (London, 1959). See also S. Tarlow, *The Archaeology of Improvement in Britain, 1750-1850* (Cambridge, 2007). Throughout the country, as Britain became more industrialised, a movement of 'Improvement' had become established where 'Improvers' set out to tame and cultivate land perceived to be wildernesses. Their intentions were to increase food production, reduce poverty and it could be argued, increase their own personal wealth.

[54] Hemery, *High Dartmoor*, p. 435: This was not the first time Frean had been given an audience with the Prince as he had previously met him to ask for permission to construct the Powdermills.

[55] It appears that the purchase was simply an investment as a year later he sold Langmoor House to Ann Farwell Moly for £3500 and a number of fields to John

Wilcocks for £2000. By 1863 he still owed £3750 on the property, but was in receipts of income from his houses and land in Charmouth.

[56] A. Moss and W. Valiant, *Crusade: the History of the RSPCA* (London, 1961). Amongst its earliest supporters was William Wilberforce. The society later gained royal patronage and became the RSPCA we are familiar with today.

[57] *Royal Cornwall Gazette*, 9/4/1841, p. 4.

[58] T. Crosse, *Cherrybrook Rose* (Sutton, 2008), p. 76.

[59] Frean's departure may have been part of a process of 'slowing down' as he got older. See the *Royal Cornwall Gazette*, 17/10/1851, p. 8, for the announcement that George Frean was retiring from being a member of the Plymouth Town Council.

[60] The Duchy Archives, George Frean's letter to Mr Barrington', (135), 11/5/1866.

[61] See also the *Western Times,* 19/4/1851, p. 3: 'Cultivation of Dartmoor and Use of Peat.—At a recent meeting of the Devon and Cornwall Natural History Society, Mr. George Frean, of Plymouth, introduced the subject of the use and application of Peat'.

[62] His wife is recorded as dying a year later.

[63] Somers Cocks, *Dartmoor: A New Study*, p. 258.

[64] *Western Times*, 10/1/1857, p. 6.

[65] Kennall Mills, began producing gunpowder in 1812. By the 1860s the Kennall Company was employing over fifty people. It was one of two works in Cornwall, the other being at the nearby Cosawes Wood, which was taken over by the Kennall Company.

[66] *Oxford University, City and County Herald*, 9/11/1845. The tone of the report and its reference to specific measurements concerning the sites distance to settlements and the nearest road, suggests that some people had concerns about the dangers of making gunpowder and may have actively opposed it.

[67] See Anon, 'Historical Weather Events'. http://booty.org.uk/booty.weather/climate/1800_1849.htm (30/6/16).

[68] P. Heath, *Melbourne 1820-1875: A Diary by John Joseph Briggs* (Derby, 2005), p. 38.

[69] *The Gentleman's Magazine*, 178, 1845 Jan-Jun., p. 415.

[70] Brunton, *The Gunpowder Mills: Dartmoor*, p. 3. See Anon, 'Peek Freans.' https://en.wikipedia.org/wiki/Peek_Freans (25/6/16). See also Anon, 'Bank of England Inflation Calculator.' http://www.bankofengland.co.uk/education/Pages/resources/inflationtools/calculator/default.aspx (05/07/2017).

[71] We cannot say for sure what caused Frean to take such action. He may not have been able to raise the required funds. He may not have been prepared to risk

any more capital on the project. Or it may have always have been his intention to finance the project in this manner – after all many of his prior investments involved partnerships. See Anon, 'Peek Freans.' https://en.wikipedia.org/wiki/Peek_Freans (25/6/16).

[72] The company was not a joint stock company where actual shares were created for people to invest in the company, it was simply a business that was owned by a collective. For nineteenth century joint stock companies see H. Perkins, *Origins of Modern English Society, 1780-1880* (1969, London, 1972), p. 116.

[73] *Western Times*, 22/11/1845, p. 5.

[74] I am grateful to Terry Rounsefell for his analysis of the newspaper reports concerning the partnerships that owned the Plymouth and Dartmoor Gunpowder Company.

[75] *London Gazette*, 3/9/1847, pp. 3214-5.

[76] Ashford, 'Some thoughts on Dartmoor Powder Mills', p. 63.

[77] *Western Times*, 3/7/1852, p. 6: This was a report on the theft of gunpowder from the company.

[78] The company also published the *Plymouth and Devonport Weekly Journal.*

[79] See T.L. Alborn, *Conceiving Companies: Joint-Stock Politics in Victorian England* (London, 1998) regarding W.D. Rubinstein's claim that 'British economic power has always rested in the gentlemanly sectors of financial service and international trade', further describing these gentlemen as 'having prospered through by jettisoning their Georgian predecessors' infamous inefficiencies', p. 11.

[80] Perkins, *Origins of Modern English Society,* p. 51: '"County society" was a real entity, a comparatively small, face to face group of personal acquaintances'. Perkins further argues that industrialism was born out of a 'wide diffusion of modest wealth' combined with a 'system of kinship and connection which could reinforce the individual's capital from the resources of a wide range of friends and relations', p. 80. See also Alborn, *Conceiving Companies,* p. 10, regarding how nineteenth-century capitalists 'consolidated their power through kinship ties and public-school friendships'.

[81] It's also possible that the investors selling their shares wanted to put their capital into other ventures or they'd fallen on hard times.

[82] See Adams and others versus Dale, The Charlestown United Mines, St Austell, Vicewarden's Court of Stannaries of Devon and Cornwall, STA/693c/588.

[83] W. Monk (ed.), *Journals of Caroline Fox from 1835-1871* (London, 1972), p. 219.

[84] While contemporary newspapers reported when company partnerships ended,

they rarely inform us of exactly when new partners join existing companies.

[85] *London Evening Standard*, 22/6/1869, p. 8.

[86] I am grateful to Roderick Martin for his help in researching the Williams family.

[87] I am grateful to Dr Steve Childs for his help in researching the Williams family.

[88] See Chapter 5 for a more detailed account of Charles Williams Jnr.

[89] It is possible that other people may have been partners in the company but there involvement was never recorded by the newspaper.

[90] R.N. Worth, *The History of Plymouth from the Earliest Period to the Present Time* (Plymouth, 1873), p. 255: 'The Plymouth and Dartmoor Gunpowder Company has its works on Dartmoor, but its offices in Plymouth'.

[91] To date it has not been possible to find a map showing Sunnyside Cottages; however, these buildings are referred to in letters kept at the Duchy Office.

[92] The Lobb family had Elizabeth Martin living with them who may have been a servant.

[93] M. Anderson 'The social implication of demographic change' in F.M.L. Thompson (ed.), *The Cambridge Social History of Britain 1750-1950, Volume II: People and their Environment* (Cambridge, 1990), p. 11.

[94] For many people at this time, an outsider was someone who lived more than five miles away. See K.D.M. Snell, *Parish and Belonging: Community, Identity and Welfare in England and Wales, 1700-1950* (Cambridge, 2006), p. 43: 'In a village, as Ronald Blythe wrote of East Anglia, a "foreigner" came from five miles down the road – "make no bones about it, six miles from us it is all another country"'.

[95] W. Crossing writing in 1901 claimed that due to the remoteness of the area 'the morals of the moor people were less likely to be corrupted, although it is certain that their standard was by no means a high one'. See Crossing, *A Hundred Years on Dartmoor*, p. 94.

[96] Thomas the Carter and his wife were lodging with the Daws in 1851, but ten years on they are no longer lodgers and now have their own house.

[97] Some workers lived off-site but then moved into workers' accommodation. For example, in 1851 Samuel Cooper is listed as a labourer living at Cherrybrook Bridge. Ten years later he is listed as a carter at the factory with his wife and six children, of whom the youngest is Susan, aged six months. Also Frederick King is recorded as living at Cherrybook Bridge and is described as a cooper from Ashburton aged twenty-three. Ten years later he is living at the Powdermills with his wife and four sons with Frederick Jnr also employed as a cooper. In 1871 Frederick and his son Frederick Jnr are both still listed as coopers and living at Powdermills.

[98] P. Joyce, 'Work' in F.M.L. Thompson (ed.), *The Cambridge Social History of Britain*

1750-1950, Volume II: People and their Environment (Cambridge, 1990), p. 139: 'Mobility was probably at its height between 1840 and 1890…More than three quarters of the population of Manchester, Bradford and Glasgow aged 20 years and over in 1851 were born outside these cities'.

[99] A. Briggs, *A Social History of Britain* (1983, London, 1987), p. 286.

[100] The Duchy Archives, Fire insurance policy no 3711017, The North Briton and Merwhite Insurance Co. 19/10/1907. In this cluster of buildings there is only one detached building shown on contemporary maps, that being the present Pottery Café.

[101] This phrase is also used to describe the weather in Scotland.

[102] G. Crocker, *The Gunpowder Industry* (Haverfordwest, 2002), p. 20. The cooperage is where the gunpowder barrels were made. The majority of gunpowder works made their own barrels where a large proportion of the company's workforce would be employed.

[103] Brunton, *The Gunpowder Mills: Dartmoor*, p. 15.

[104] Best, *Mid-Victorian Britain*, p. 119. These figures are for England and Wales.

[105] L. Davidoff, 'The family in Britain' in F.M.L. Thompson (ed.), *The Cambridge Social History of Britain 1750-1950, Volume II: People and their Environment* (Cambridge, 1990), p. 113.

[106] L. Davidoff, 'The family in Britain' in F.M.L. Thompson (ed.), *The Cambridge Social History of Britain 1750-1950, Volume II: People and their Environment* (Cambridge, 1990), pp. 112-22. K.D.M. Snell, *Annals of the Labouring Poor: Social Change and Agrarian England 1660-1900* (Cambridge, 1985), p. 371: 'Women had largely withdrawn from field work and their occupation by 1850 had become strictly that of "housewife"'.

[107] Anderson, 'The social implication of demographic change', p. 64.

[108] *Western Times,* 5/10/1877, p. 7. Jane James was forty eight years old. She is listed in the 1871 census as being originally from Lezant in Cornwall, married to William James (64) a 'Gunpowder Maker' with two children Mary (28) and Thomas (23).

[109] I am grateful to Dr Steve Childs for drawing my attention to the detail and outcome of the trial in 1878 and additional information concerning the Williams and Bellamy families.

[110] The 1911 census lists Charles Francis living with his wife Emily and two children in Princetown.

[111] T. Greeves and E. Stanbrook, *The Warren House Inn, Dartmoor* (2001, Brixham, 2004), p. 8. Originally the pub was called the New House.

[112] Ten years later, in 1871, Jonas Coaker is described as a retired farmer. For a nineteenth century account of the poet Jonas Coaker see: W.H.K. Wright, *West-Country Poets: Their Lives and Works* (London, 1986), pp. 99-101. See also S. Baring-Gould, *Dartmoor Idles* (London, 1896), pp. 138-155.

[113] W. J. Webb, *Devonshire Scenery: Its Inspiration in the Prose and Song of Various Authors* (Exeter, 1884), pp. 103-4.

[114] Wright, *West Country Poets*, p. 99.

[115] It is also worth noting that the evidence is from censuses taken every ten years and there may have been some years when the numbers employed were greater than those of 1861, but still it is difficult to imagine that one of these years could have recorded employment levels of 100.

[116] The term children refers to the offspring of the householders. Nearly all of these were under eighteen (the majority under 10). Some were what we refer to as 'young adults' (over 18): 1851 – 1, 1861 – 0, 1871 – 3, 1881 – 3, 1891 – 1.

[117] By 1861 he is listed as living at Cosowes Woods in Cornwall with his wife and three daughters. He is described as gunpowder maker.

[118] James Lobb is recorded as living at the Powdermills in the 1851 census with his wife Charity.

[119] J. Ewan, 'William Lobb, plant hunter for Veitch and messenger of the big tree', *University of California Press,* 67-8, (1978).

[120] *London Gazette*, 8/11/1861, p. 4474.

[121] Unfortunately we do not have the details of the changes.

[122] James is recorded as living at 10, Clifton Place, Plymouth.

[123] *London Evening Standard*, 22/6/1869, p. 8. In this report concerning the company it refers to their offices in Plymouth.

[124] *The Tavistock Gazette,* 15/3/1872.

[125] Before moving to Powdermills the census returns reveal that in 1851 Robert, his wife and daughter Jessie lived in Yealmpton where he was employed as a sawyer. The family then moved to the Saw Mills in Ermington c.1852 where Robert continued to work as a sawyer. The census for 1861 records Robert and his wife Mary still living in Ermington with their six children. Mary gave birth to at least eleven children.

[126] *Western Morning News*, 10/5/1882, p. 2.

[127] *The Era,* 27/7/1885.

[128] *Exeter and Plymouth Gazette*, 9/4/1886, p. 5.

[129] *Royal Cornwall Gazette*, 13/7/1849, pp. 6-7. In this report George Frean states

that the company are aware of the laws concerning storage of gunpowder and adhere to them.

[130] The position of the magazine was however, close to the Powder Mills Cottages West.

[131] *Royal Cornwall Gazette*, 13/7/1849, pp. 6-7. This indicates there were possibly other magazines, however he may have been including the stores which were also on site and held unfinished gunpowder.

[132] *London Evening Standard*, 22/6/1869, p. 8. This report refers to the company's magazine in Wales.

[133] R. Groves, 'Roads and Tracks' in C. Gill (ed.), *Dartmoor: A New Study* (Newton Abbot, 1977). Writing in 1901 William Crossing makes the following observation: 'Dartmoor roads are all good, there being in such a district no lack of suitable material for their repair'. See Crossing, *A Hundred Years on Dartmoor*, p. 47.

[134] Snow drifts and flooding are a constant problem on the moor. See Crossing, *A Hundred Years on Dartmoor*, pp.145-7, regarding numerous accounts of people perishing in the snow such as the three Royal Fusiliers in 1853.

[135] *Western Courier, West of England Conservative Plymouth and Devonport Advertiser*, 19/5/1852. Cudlip had been arrested for being in possession of gunpowder without any documentation and confessed to receiving the stolen goods from Rowe and Hill. *See Western Courier, West of England Conservative Plymouth and Davenport Advertiser*, 21/4/1854, p. 5, for a report where Mr T.B. Tyeth (Secretary to the Company), claims that gunpowder worth £3150.00 was missing.

[136] *Western Times*, 3/7/1852, p. 6.

[137] *Woolmer's Exeter and Plymouth Gazette*, 8/6/1848, p. 8. R.S. Lambert, *The Cobbet of the West: A Study of Thomas Latimer and the Struggle between Pulpit and Press at Exeter* (London, 1939), p. 42: Edward Woolmer was the 'proprietor of the Exeter and Plymouth Gazette, one of the best-known journals in the country. Woolmer was a Tory, a member of the Exeter Corporation and inside the ring of Exeter vested interests'. Clearly the magazine was not in his or his associates' interest.

[138] L. James, *The Middle Class: A History* (London, 2006), p. 297.

[139] *Western Times*, 22/7/1848, p. 3. Lambert, *Cobbet of the West*, pp. 50-3: 'The Western Times was a poorer periodical than the Gazette: its circulation was little over a thousand: its paper thin and its advertising vulgar...Still it was definitely Radical'. The paper appealed to 'the tradesman and shopkeeper, the tenant farmer and craftsman'.

[140] *Woolmer's Exeter and Plymouth Gazette*, 5/8/1848, p. 8.

[141] *Woolmer's Exeter and Plymouth Gazette,* 14/10/1848, p. 8.

[142] *Western Times*, 21/10/1848, p. 3.

[143] *Royal Cornwall Gazette*, 13/7/1849, pp. 6-7. The licence was granted to the East Cornwall Gunpowder Company for a factory at Treago Wood in the parish of St Pinnock on conditions.

[144] *South Wales Daily News,* 25/8/1877, p. 1. Originally the gunpowder company wanted to lease a magazine in the Cornish parish of Gwennap in the manor of Cusgarne but there was sufficient opposition to thwart them. See *Royal Cornwall Gazette,* 13/4/1849, p. 6.

[145] See *London Evening Standard*, 22/6/1869, p. 8 and A.R. Pye, 'An Example of a Non-metalliferous Dartmoor Industry: the Gunpowder Factory at Powdermills', in D.M. Griffiths (ed.) *The Archaeology of Dartmoor: Perspectives from the 1990's* (Stroud, 1996), p. 221.

[146] Gunpowder agent and gunpowder merchant appears to be the same job, therefore to avoid confusion this study will use the term agent.

[147] The census returns for England and Wales between 1851-91 record few gunpowder agents. The numbers are as follows: 1851 - 2, 1861 - 3, 1871 - 7, 1881 - 4, 1891 - 1.

[148] Perhaps no longer being a partner in the company prevented him from negotiating a favourable deal. It may have been the case that when the Williams took over the company it became less profitable selling gunpowder for Tyeth. However, this is pure speculation and it may have been the case that he just decided it was time to retire.

[149] *Royal Cornwall Gazette*, 24/2/1872, p. 1.

[150] To make things even more complicated it transpires that Webb's dealings were not with the fuse company direct but with an agent named Willoughby who was representing Brunton and Co.

[151] *West Briton and Cornwall Advertiser*, 7/11/1862, p. 4.

[152] On the same page it was reported that a petition to close the South Wheal Kitty Mine (where Webb was employed as purser) had been made as they were in debt £700. This leads us to wonder whether Webb was in any way responsible for their financial problems. Being employed by these mines meant it would have been easy to sell the fuses to them.

[153] Webb had ceased delivering paperwork to the company between 1860 and 1862 and claimed that what paperwork he had, had been given to the Exeter District Court of Bankruptcy.

[154] Thomas B. Tyeth was born in Launceston, Cornwall in 1802.

[155] *Dorset County Chronicle*, 14/2/1884.

[156] Harris, *The Industrial Archaeology of Dartmoor*.

[157] Pye, 'An Example of a Non-metalliferous Dartmoor Industry', p. 221.

[158] Ashford, 'Some thoughts on Dartmoor Powder Mills', p. 67. See also B. Ashford, 'A new interpretation of the historical data on the gunpowder industry in Devon and Cornwall', *The Trevithick Society*, 43 (2016), pp. 65–73. See p. 68 and p. 72, concerning the issue of whether it was sodium or potassium nitrate that was used.

[159] See the *Oxford University, City and County Herald*, 9/11/1844, p. 2, regarding the beginning of the factory's construction and the *Western Times*, 22/11/1845, p. 5, for its opening. Other buildings would have been added and additional ones given different uses as the company attempted to find the most efficient way of making gunpowder.

[160] English Heritage, 'Gunpowder factory at Powder Mills'. http://www.heritagegateway.org.uk/Gateway/Results_Single.aspx?uid=MDV43177&resource ID=104 (19/01/2017).

[161] Unfortunately no timber work remains on site. It has either been taken to be recycled by locals or used as firewood by the American soldiers that were stationed there during World War II.

[162] We have yet to establish whether the charcoal was made on site or brought in. Regarding the Sicilian sulphur and South American potassium nitrate, the company may have traded with suppliers oversees. If so, these raw materials would have been shipped to Plymouth, where they would have been unloaded and taken by horse drawn railway to Princetown and then transported by horse and cart to the Powdermills. However, during conversations with Bob Ashford he made the point that these materials were commercially available in this country and may have been purchased from individuals or companies who supplied them.

[163] English Heritage, 'Gunpowder factory at Powder Mills'. http://www.heritagegateway.org.uk/Gateway/Results_Single.aspx?uid=MDV43177&resource ID=104 (19/01/2017. For a more detailed description of how the factory operated, see Ashford, 'Some thoughts on Dartmoor Powder Mills', pp. 71-80.

[164] Ashford, 'Some thoughts on Dartmoor Powder Mills', pp. 63-7. Ashford calculates that the factory had the potential for making approx. 300 tonnes a year, p. 71.

[165] For the1872 inspection see the *Tavistock Gazette* 15/3/1872.

[166] J.J. Hainsworth, *Jack the Ripper – Case Solved, 1891* (Jefferson, N. Carolina, USA, 2015), pp. 86-105. The Druitt and Majendie families were very close.

[167] *Tavistock Gazette*, 15/03/1872.

[168] W.D. Cocroft, *Dangerous Energy, the Archaeology of Gunpowder and Military Explosives Manufacture* (London, 1999), pp. 98-9.

[169] *Dorset County Chronicle*, 14/2/1884, p. 14. There was a further explosion in February 1887. I am grateful to Roderick Martin for pointing this out to me.

[170] In 1911 eleven people are recorded as living at Powdermills.

[171] The Bellamy's were loosely related to Charles Williams as William Bellamy had married Charles' cousin's daughter (Chapter 4).

[172] The Duchy Archives, 'Charles Williams letter to the Duchy land steward', (362) 20/4/1903.

[173] The Duchy Archives, 'Charles Williams letter to A.E. Barrington', (379) 8/ 8/ 1903.

[174] The Duchy Archives, 'Charles Williams letter to the Duchy office', (362) 15/71907. This letter was also written from the Plymouth theatre. In the same year Williams took out fire insurance with North British and Merwhite Insurance Co where they valued the buildings at £1,400.

[175] The Duchy Archives, 'Letter from J.C. Revell (representing Miss Pearse)', (279) 20/9/1917.

[176] See the Duchy Archives for correspondence between these individuals and the Duchy office. Letters not numbered.

[177] Tim Cumming / The Rowley Gallery 'From Powdermills to Wistmans Wood', http://blog.rowleygallery.co.uk/from-powdermills-to-wistmans-wood/ (08/05/2017).

[178] C. Taylor's quotes are taken from his introduction to W.G. Hoskins, *The Making of the English Landscape* (1955, London, 1988), p. 8.

[179] Hoskins, *Making of the English Landscape,* p. 9. C. Taylor describes the first revolution as during the later Bronze Age 'around 1800-1400 BC', p. 8, and the second revolution being during the latter part of the Saxon period, p. 9.

[180] I am grateful to Tom Greeves for drawing these millstones to my attention. Tom photographed three of these millstones in 2014. The rockery/patio belonged to John and Liz Vale at Hartyland in Postbridge. A fourth one has been made into a fountain. It is believed that Mrs Pethybridge acquired them in the 1930's.

[181] See J.M. Martin, 'The Parliamentary enclosure movement and rural society in Warwickshire', *Agricultural History Review*, 15 (1967), for a good example of how 'improvements' impacted on the local politics of an area.

[182] Some of the factory's workings have been taken off-site and are being used for other purposes such as the millstones found in the patio at Postbridge.

[183] A.R. Pye, 'An example of a non-metalliferous Dartmoor industry: the gunpowder

factory at Powdermills', in D.M. Griffiths (ed.) *The Archaeology of Dartmoor: Perspectives from the 1990s* (Stroud, 1996), B. Ashford, 'Some thoughts on Dartmoor Powder Mills', *The Devonshire Association for the Advancement of Science, Literature and the Arts*, 146 (2014), B. Ashford, 'Further Thoughts on Dartmoor Powdermills', *Transactions of the Devonshire Association for the Advancement of Science, Literature and the Arts*, 149 (2017), pp. 37–46. See also Pye, and R. Robinson, 'An Archaeological Survey of the Gunpowder Factory at Powdermills Farm, Postbridge, Dartmoor, Devon', *Exeter Museums Archaeological Field Unit Report,* 7 (1990) and T. Dawson and J. Hambly 'An Archaeological Survey of the Ancillary Buildings belonging to the Powdermills Gunpowder Factory, Postbridge', *Exeter Archaeology Report,* 63 (1995). These studies provide a much more detailed analysis of the science and archaeology concerning the site.

[184] Even though the Powdermills is often referred to as a factory, it is important to note that it was not a conventional factory i.e. one large building in which numerous processes occurred and the majority of the workforce was employed. As we have already established it was a number of small buildings spread out over a large site.

[185] It is worth noting that the 1885 map shows a substantial building just before you get to the gate on the left. This may have been living quarters for workers who may also have provided the site with around the clock security. Today nothing remains of this structure.

[186] The gunpowder was moved along the track, past the residential buildings and on to the company magazine.

[187] The 1885 map reveals that a track existed closer to the buildings upon which the raw materials were transported as they moved down the production line. Evidence of this can still be seen and in some places it has been supported by a wall which prevents it from slipping down the slope. The road that runs through the site today has clearly been maintained (presumably by farmers), but this is not a new road as a track following the same line is also shown on the 1885 map. This was presumably the road upon which the finished goods where taken out.

[188] The 1885 map shows a path leading from the workers' accommodation to the Checking House and then down to the factory site. Clearly this was the route the on-site employees took to get to work. But not all employees lived on-site. For the workers coming in from Postbridge the easiest and quickest route would have been to cut across the field from the main road to access the works near the three incorporation mills. There is a well-worn path there today and this short cut would

have saved approximately 20 minutes on their walk to work. However, this would have meant accessing the factory without any checks carried out. It may have been the case that off-site workers were made to enter the works via the checking house but left work taking the short cut (this is presuming there wasn't a signing out procedure). Another possibility is that Postbridge workers may have been brought in by horse and cart and therefore entering and leaving the site in the correct manner wasn't that much of an issue for them.

[189] See Pye, 'An Example of a Non-metalliferous Dartmoor Industry', p. 226.

[190] Of the three mills, the middle one is different in design. B. Ashford suggests that this may have been a later addition. See Ashford, 'Some thoughts on Dartmoor Powder Mills', p. 73.

[191] Pye, 'An Example of a Non-metalliferous Dartmoor Industry', p. 239. The idea that charcoal could have been made is supported by the presence of willow near the cottages.

[192] Ashford, 'Further Thoughts on Dartmoor Powdermills', pp. 37-46.

[193] Analysis of the Domesday Book reveals that the small number of settlements that record having mills are mostly placed in the south west of the moor. It is not known why this is.

[194] It's possible that the water from the reservoirs was to be used to put out fires.

[195] Most maps show just two reservoirs, however, Pye's 1989 site plan reveals a third one behind the second incorporation mill. See Pye, An Example of a Non-metalliferous Dartmoor Industry, p. 223.

[196] Hemery, *High Dartmoor*, p. 436.

INDEX

M

Macnaghton, Sir Melville 86
Magazines 31, 44, 65, 69, 75, 77, 78,
     79, 84, 89, 102, 104, 119
Majendie
   Colonel Vivian Dering 72, 83, 86, 87,
     88, 122
Manager 8, 10, 17, 33, 34, 41, 43, 45,
     50, 51, 52, 53, 59, 60, 61, 62,
     66, 69, 70, 71, 72, 73, 74, 79,
     87, 91, 92, 95
Martin
   Catherine 52
   Elizabeth 50
   Household 51, 59, 62, 70
   James 52, 69, 70
   Jane 69
   Maryann 52, 69
   Roderick 4, 61, 73, 116, 122
Masons 18
Messrs Brunton and Co 80
Michell, Ralph 93
Milliman
   Household 53, 59, 61
   John 57
   Mary 57
Millstones 84, 95, 122
Monkey Puzzle tree 70, 91
Mortimer, Elizabeth 56
Mortimore, Household 53
Mouse, Household 59

N

New Inn 24
Northcott 50
   Elizabeth 50
   Household 51, 52
   Robert 50

P

Paddy, Francis 52, 69, 70
Parr, James 57, 59
Pearce, Edward 80
Pearse, Miss L.M. 93, 122
Peek Freans 28, 114, 115
Perran Wharf ironworks 43
Picken, Samuel 47

Polkinhorn, William 42, 47
Powder maker 59, 61, 66
Powdermill Cottages 49, 51
Prince Albert 30, 31, 91
Princetown 4, 19, 29, 44, 49, 54, 57,
     59, 60, 61, 84, 89, 113, 117,
     121
Pulleyblank, Frederick 55
Pye, Andrew 97, 104

Q

Queen Victoria 31, 91, 92

R

Ridgway Saw Mills, Plympton 74
River Dart 40, 106
Rowe, John 76
Rowse
   George 22
   Thomas 17
Rundle, Richard 47

S

Saltoun, Mr 93
Saracen's Head Hotel 24
School 10, 53, 54, 75, 91, 115
Schultze Gunpowder Factory 25,
     110, 112
Slee, Household 59, 61
Sleep, Silas 16, 17, 110
Smith
   Captain 72, 73
   Household 59
   Joseph 50
   Mrs 93
Soady, Thomas Eales 42, 47
Society for the Prevention of Cruelty to
     Animals 32
Soper, Eliana 47
Sparrow
   Benjamin 42
   John Wakeham 42
Spur, Henrietta 45
Stephens
   George 17
   Mr 64
   R.G. 64